IT MUST BE TRUE:
Paw-Paw Said So

Alan Easley

NukeWorks
Publishing

NukeWorks Publishing
Fulton, Mo 65251 USA

Copyright © 2013 Alan Easley

ISBN 978-0-9825294-7-8

All rights reserved. No part of this book may be used or reproduced in any manner whatsoever without written permission, except in the case of brief quotations embodied in critical articles and reviews.

Cover design by Justin Easley

Cover Photos by Kile Brewer, used with permission of the photographer and the Columbia Missourian

Author photo by Lewis Baumgartner, "Worlds Worst Farmer"

Quote from the book "Swappin' Cattle" by Wade Choate used with permission of Wade Choate.

Illustration of "Carol's Britches" by James Bratten www.skinnyd.com

All other photos used with permission of their respective owners.

Printed in U.S.A.

In Loving Memory

Marcia Easley
1943 - 2012

ACKNOWLEDGMENTS

Many thanks to Justin and Kadi, without their help this book would never have seen daylight. Also, thanks to Dolores McCray for deciphering my chicken scratching and putting it in shape for Justin and Kadi. Special thanks to Marcia for bunches of moral support, and to all other family members and friends who said "Go for it." And most of all, thanks to everyone mentioned in this book. If they hadn't done the things they did there wouldn't have been anything to write about. When I started working on this book it never entered my mind that I could be dedicating it to Marcia's memory, but things don't always go as planned. Baby, this is for you. You made the past 50-some years worthwhile, I love you!

INTRODUCTION

I was raised on a farm located about five miles south of Columbia, Missouri, that has been in the family since the 1840s. Pappy was raised there, Grandpap was raised there, and his Pap built a log cabin on the farm and moved there with his new bride in the early 1860s. Our son Jeff now lives in the old farm house which was built in the 1870s, so five generations of Easley's have lived on the farm over the years. I still raise cattle on the place, even though it is now surrounded by the City Limits of Columbia on 3-and-a-half sides.

The stories in this book range from things that occurred when Grandpap was a boy to some fairly recent events. I hope you enjoy reading about them as much as I have enjoyed remembering them and writing them down.

I'm sure I've failed to mention some people who should have been mentioned, however it was totally inadvertent. If I've stepped on anyone's toes, that could have been totally inadvertent also, or I might have done it on purpose, it just depends on who it was and how hard I stepped. Either way, "It Must Be True: Paw-Paw Said So."

The Old Neighborhood	15
Grandpap and Grandma	29
Charlie Richardson	41
Model "T" Fords	43
Dr. Nifong and "Miss Lavinia"	47
Hog Killing	53
Walkup's Station	61
Growing Up in the 1950s	65
Pappy and Momma	83
Guns and Hunting, and Fishing Too	95
Traveling Salesmen and Pass-Through Painters	103
School Boards	107
Tractors, Machinery, and Machinery Dealers	111
Olivet Neighbors	121
Kids	149
Norm Beal	157
Party Lines	159
Carol's Britches	161
Country Churches, Preachers, BAR-B-Q's and Fish Fry's	163
Damn Sewer Lines	173
Damn Trespassers	179
4-H Calves 4-H Leaders	185
Grandkids	189
Worthless Old Horses	201
Me, Bill, and Beer	205
The Fortney Cemetery	211
Putting Up Hay	213
MFA (Missouri Farmers Association)	225
Random Thoughts and Other Things	237

IT MUST BE TRUE:
Paw-Paw Said So

The Old Neighborhood

    The neighborhood south of Columbia where I grew up sure has changed over the years. When I was a kid we had lots of neighbors around the old place. Some of them lived 8 or 10 miles away, but they were considered neighbors. Now there are lots of people, but very few real neighbors.

    Just north of the house the Nifong property became Woodhaven Children's Home, which wasn't a very desirable neighbor. They eventually sold out to Boys and Girls Town, which isn't any improvement. North of Boys and Girls Town the Nifong place is covered with 4-plexes, duplexes, and mobile homes all the way to Grindstone Parkway. Pappy farmed this property for years, and when I was a kid I spent a lot of hours working this ground with an 8N Ford tractor. I baled hay off of part of it for several years after I started farming.

    The old Frank Hall place has duplexes and 4-plexes built so close together that the houses share driveways. Pappy rented part of this farm when I was a kid, and I rented it from the Hall heirs for 13 years, back in the 1960s and early '70's. It wasn't the best ground in the world, but it's where I got started farming.

    The property that I rented from Hale and Glydas Cavcey for pasture and hay is now covered with cookie-cutter houses, even down to the same color paint.

    The Gregory place has some really nice looking smaller homes on it, but the developers made a hell of a mess out of the property before they started building. They didn't have enough sense to go with the lay of the land, they blasted 10 to 20 feet of solid rock off the hill tops before they ever started building streets.

Joe Crane's farm is split into 10 and 20 acre tracts, and of course Elvin Sapp is developing the Phillips property. He has built some really nice houses towards the West side, on the East side there is a Catholic High School, and there would have been a bunch of commercial development by now, if the economy hadn't gotten Obama'd. The streets are already built, so I guess that will still happen eventually.

Tom and Jim Watson still own their place on Gans Road. Neither one lives there, but Tom comes out pretty regularly. Tommy Stewart still lives on the place T. B. bought back in the 1950s, north of Charlie Hall's place, which is now part of Rock Bridge State Park. Jimmy Stewart rents the old Steve Shelden place from Maxine Glenn. Maxine has sold the farm to Rock Bridge Park, but reserved use of it for her lifetime. I see Jimmy occasionally, when I go up to the Fortney Cemetery.

Tommy Stewart and his mules, 2008. Tommy has been a neighbor for nearly 60 years.

Beatrice Judd still lives on Rock Quarry Road, she's the last of the old time neighbors. Tom and Carol Norling live at the corner of Gans Road and Rock Quarry. I don't hardly ever see them, but I know where they are if I need them. They slip down the road fairly regularly and check on Beatrice. The neighbor thing never quits completely, it just sort of changes over the years.

Fred and Kathy Vom Saal have several acres of the Joe Crane Place, and Mom sold them two acres off of her place about a year before she died. Fred and Kathy were really good to Mom when she lived alone on the farm, and they are definitely considered neighbors.

Joe and Corriene Remieke live in the Bearfield Subdivision, and they used to visit with mom when she lived on the farm, but I haven't seen them more than a couple of times since mom died. There are a few others that I know by name, and we wave when we see each other, but they're not really neighbors in the old time sense of the word.

When mom lived by herself we had lots of trespassers on the farm, and some son-of-a-bitch even cooked off a batch of meth in the barn one night, and left the aftermath. Jeff lives in the old house now, and people have discovered that he isn't really nice when he finds uninvited guests, so trespassing isn't nearly as much of a problem anymore.

I guess most of this is considered progress, but as far as I'm concerned it just screwed up some good pasture ground and deer woods. I liked it a hell of a lot better the way it was before.

* * * * *

One time I was helping Joe Crane rebuild some fence. We were stretching the wire with Joe's little

Farmall "C," and we had a barb wire stretched and were getting ready to staple it to a tree in the fence row. Joe had grabbed the wire with both hands to push it against the tree when it slipped out of the stretcher. About 2 and-a-half feet of wire ripped through Joe's hands. He was wearing leather gloves, but it still got quite a bit of meat. We went to the house and Joe washed his hands in kerosene, then Meda wrapped them in gauze. Joe decided we'd take the rest of the day off.

The next morning as I walked across Joe's yard, just before 7:00 A.M., Joe called out "Have a seat, I'll be out as soon as I finish mopping the porch." That was Joe's job, and Meda didn't see any reason why he shouldn't do it, just because his hands were a little sore.

* * * * *

In 1954 there was a really bad drought. Pappy said it wasn't as bad as 1934, but he claimed it was worse than 1980. I don't remember it that well, but it must have been something if it was worse than 1980. '80 didn't break me, but it sure bent the hell out of me.

Anyhow, in 1954 Little Bill Brynjulfson (who was a lot bigger than Old Bill) took the sides off his grain truck, mounted a 1000 gallon tank, and started hauling stock water. He bought a pump and some hose, and pumped water out of Grindstone Creek. He pumped it and hauled it for $3.00 per load. That doesn't sound like much, but when he dumped 1000 gallons in a pond that had gone dry it didn't last long. Bill made some money that summer, and kept a lot of cattle and hogs alive that would have gone to slaughter otherwise. If you wanted to do that now, by the time you could get a permit from the damn EPA to pump water out of a creek, the drought would be over.

It Must Be True: Paw-Paw Said So

* * * * *

Mom told me that not too many years after her and Pappy got married, Jap Willingham and his family moved to the farm on Gans Road that Watson's now own. Mom said that he made it pretty clear that he didn't come into the neighborhood to bother anyone, and that he didn't want a bunch of people bothering him. People thought that was a little strange, because back then neighbors made a habit of helping each other, but everyone figured if that was how he wanted it, it was fine with them, so that's how it was until one day that fall.

Pappy had taken his tractor and cut-off saw to Charlie Hall's, and then Doc Fortney's, as he and Grandpap helped them saw their winters wood. After they finished at Doc's they were standing around the saw, sampling Doc's homemade wine, when someone remarked "you know, that Willingham feller has a big pile of wood up, but he's been really sick and hasn't got any of it cut into stove wood."

After a short discussion it was decided that there was enough daylight left and they had plenty of help, so they were going to saw Willingham's wood whether he wanted to be bothered or not. No one was home when they arrived, so they set up, sawed the woodpile, and left without ever seeing anyone.

Mom said 2 or 3 weeks went by and no-one had heard anything about the wood sawing. One morning Pappy, Grandpap, and Charlie Richardson were shucking corn in a field by the road when Willingham drove past. Right after dinner he showed up at the field and said "I thought I'd help you all shuck for a while, if that's all right." Mom said he worked that afternoon, and then worked all day for the next two days. As he was leaving on the last day he asked, "William, who helped you and your pap saw my wood?" Pappy told him, and he shucked corn for two of them that fall, and showed up and pitched hay for the other two the next summer.

Mom said he never came right out and said thank you to anyone, but he made sure that everyone was well paid back. She said that afterwards, if someone needed help, Willingham was always the first one to show up.

* * * * *

J.W. "Wat" Cheavens and his hound dog Robbie, 1963

Wat Cheavens lived just down the road from Clarence Fox for years. Clarence didn't farm enough to get by without some supplemental income, so Wat tried to give him as much work as possible. Wat farmed and also operated Cheavens Lathing and Plastering Co., so he would work Clarence on the farm when needed and also use him as a mud-mixer and hod carrier on construction jobs. Everyone knows that Clarence liked to take a drink occasionally. Well, actually Clarence like to take a drink pretty regularly. Actually Clarence was pretty much a drunk, but he was a hard working drunk, and as long as he was half sober he was pretty good help. No one knows how good of help he was when he was completely sober, because no-one ever saw him that way.

If you remember Clarence you know that it was pretty much impossible for him to go more than a couple of hours without a drink. One day Clarence was mixing mud for Wat at a construction site, and he had just taken a good nip from a half-pint and recapped it when he spotted Wat walking his way. He tossed the bottle in the mixer and went on with his work.

Wat visited with Clarence for a few minutes, then moved on to check with the plasterers. While he was talking to one of them, Clarence came by with a wheelbarrow full of mud and scooped 2 or 3 shovels full onto the mortar board. The last shovel full contained the bottle, still intact, with about an inch of whiskey left in the bottom. Wat picked the bottle up and wiped it off, then said "Damn, Foxey, that stuff's too expensive to throw away, if you're not going to drink it I will." Wat drained that last swallow from the bottle, re-capped it, then tossed it back into the wheelbarrow and walked away.

I don't imagine Clarence was the least bit embarrassed, but I'll bet he sure was sorry he lost that last drink of whiskey.

* * * * *

When I was a kid, Grandpap, Doc Fortney, Charlie Hall, Frank Hall, Joe Crane and everyone else in that age group always wore long sleeved shirts in the summer time, most of them with the top button fastened. They all wore wide brimmed straw hats, and some of them even wore light weight canvas gloves to keep the sun off the backs of their hands while they worked.

I would be working with no shirt and a baseball cap, and they would tell me, "Boy, get some clothes on that sun's not good for your skin." That was 40 years before doctors started telling people to stay out of the sun, so I don't know where they got their information, but they sure knew what they were talking about.

* * * * *

When Grandpap and Pappy were working in the sun they would line their hats with green leaves. Catalpa leaves worked really good, because they were so big. Tom and Jim Watson, Kenny and John Cavcey and myself started doing it too, and it really helped. As the moisture evaporates from the leaves it does a good job of cooling your head.

* * * * *

When I can first remember, Charlie Hall was the only one left in the neighborhood who still cooked with wood.

On wood sawing day Charlie always had a special pile of real small wood to cut up for the cook stove. Invariably, someone would make a comment about sawing Charlie's brush pile. Charlie would just mumble something about "You pot lickers," and keep right on carrying brush to the saw.

* * * * *

When I was a kid there was no OSHA, there weren't nearly as many greedy lawyers ready to file suit for almost any reason, and people hadn't started treating kids like delicate little flowers that must be protected at all times. Therefore, it was still possible for kids to have fun on their own.

When I was in grade school, each spring there would be an all day picnic at Charlie Hall's farm at the South end of Bearfield Road. The farm is now part of Rock Bridge State Park. On the day of the picnic, any moms who drove would stuff their cars full of kids and food, and head south to Charlie's. He would meet us in front of his house with a team and wagon. All of the food, real little kids, and any moms to fat to walk through the woods, were loaded into the wagon, and Charlie headed towards the creek with everyone else following.

When he arrived at the hay field southwest of the Mill Dam hole he would stop and unhook the wagon, then Charlie would head back to the house. The teacher and some moms laid down a few rules. Very few rules, actually. Little kids couldn't go to the creek without an adult or older child with them, 6th, 7th, and 8th graders were on their own. They were told to watch out for rattlesnakes and deep water, and told if they felt like they had to climb the bluffs to please don't fall off. Other than that, everyone was pretty much free to do as they pleased. It was always a lot of fun, and I don't remember anyone ever getting seriously hurt. Around the middle of the afternoon Charlie would return, and load the wagon for the trip back to the house.

Even if parents today would agree to turn their kids loose in such a harsh environment, it wouldn't be possible because of the tremendous liability that would be placed on the land owner.

*   *   *   *   *

One time when I was a junior in high school, and before I owned a car, I had a date one night but Pappy and Mom had some sort of meeting they wanted to attend, so I couldn't use the car. I walked up the road to Cavcey's and asked Hale if I could borrow his car. He had a big, new, white Pontiac, with the Indian head hood ornament and chrome stripes on the hood and trunk. He thought about it for a moment, then said okay, just be careful with it. That's got to be some kind of a good neighbor. Looking back, I can't believe I had the nerve to ask something like that, and I sure don't understand why he said yes.

* * * * *

After I started farming I baled hay for Hale Cavcey several times, and always hauled his calves. When he got older he couldn't take cold weather, so I fed for him for a couple of years, until he decided to sell his cows.

After he sold his cows I rented his pasture every summer. There was a gate between his place and Pappy's, so it was real handy. When Hale died and Gladys went to a nursing home, I rented the pasture from John and Kenny until they finally sold the farm. It's now covered with look-alike houses and duplexes, as close together as they could build them.

* * * * *

Like most old Boone County families, the Easley's and the Judd's are kin to each other. Guy, Beatrice and Jacquelin lived around the corner from us when I was a kid, and I knew them all my life.

Guy built houses for a living, but he was more than just a carpenter he was a true craftsman. He could build houses, cabinets, or anything else you might want.

When Marcia and I built our house in the early 1960s, I asked Guy if he had time to come by and show me how to trim the doors, windows, and etc. Guy showed up early one Saturday morning with a miter box and his hand tools. He spent the entire weekend giving me a crash course in trim carpentry. He cut all the miters with a hand saw, then worked on each piece with a small hand plane, wood rasp and sandpaper, until everything fit perfectly. Then all the pieces were hand nailed, and all the nails were countersunk with a nailset.

By late Sunday afternoon he told me that he thought I could handle the rest, and to call him if I had any problems. I was a lot slower than Guy, but I finally got the rest of the house trimmed, and it looked pretty good for a first time effort.

I kind of cringe when I watch some of today's finish carpenters. They whack off a piece of trim with a power saw, slap it into place and nail it with an air nailer. If the gap is to wide to tolerate they glob some putty into the crack and keep going. That wasn't Guy's style, he would roll over in his grave.

* * * * *

When Marcia and I lived in the little house at Wat and Thelma Cheavens' place, there was an old colored fellow who lived down towards Whoop-up and raised hogs.

That was before there were any health regulations against feeding commercial garbage to hogs, so that was pretty much all that he fed. He had a 200 gallon tank in the back of his old pickup, with a burner from an L.P. gas furnace mounted under it. Behind the cab of the truck a 100-pound L.P. bottle was wired up. When he went down the road it definitely looked like a "Sanford and Sons" operation.

He would go around town to the motels, restaurants and grocery stores and pick up their garbage, dump it in the tank, add some water if necessary, then drive slowly home while it cooked. He couldn't go very fast or the burner would blow out, so he always had a line of cars behind him.

One morning while on our way to work Marcia and I caught up with him on Route N (now Route 163) just north of Rock Quarry Road. I pulled out to pass him, and when I got along side his truck it suddenly disappeared. I looked in the mirror, and he was sitting between the road and the fence on the east side. I stopped and backed up, and when I got out I could see him laying on his back and reaching under the front of the truck. When I asked him if he was alright he replied "Yessah, I's fine, but the dammed ole tie rod juss fell off again." He raised the tie rod, lined it up, and popped it back on with one hand. As we were leaving he drove back onto the road and headed towards town.

After that, whenever I saw his old truck on the road I kind of kept my distance. I don't know how many times that tie rod had fallen off before, or how many times it fell off before he replaced it, but I'll guarantee that there were lots of places on both sides of that road where he damn sure wouldn't have wanted it to fall off, regardless of how slow he was driving.

* * * * *

When I was growing up the neighbors called the road in front of the house "Easley Lane," and we called it "Home Road." When Dave Bear bought the 20 acre strip south of Doc Fortney's and developed Bearfield Subdivision, he petitioned the County Commission to name the road "Bearfield Road." Pappy and I were talking about it, and I remarked that Dave was the last person to buy property along the road, and that he owned fewer acres that anyone else.

I suggested that Pappy go to the commission meeting and protest the suggested name. He replied "Oh, Alan, if it makes Mr. Bear feel important to have a road named after him, I'm not going to try to stop it from happening."

I guess Pappy was a lot mellower than I am, because it still gripes my butt every time I see those road signs.

Three views of the Easley House. 1940, 1966, and showing it's age in 2012.

Grandpap and Grandma

When Grandpap was born in 1865 most of the farm was still in virgin timber. His dad and uncle cleared part of it, and Grandpap cleared a lot more after he was grown.

One summer when he was around six or seven years old, his dad, his uncle, and a couple of hired men were clearing a field just east of the log cabin in which the family lived. There wasn't much market for saw logs, and there was a limit to how many rails were needed, so except for a few prime logs after the trees were cut and limbed they were drug into piles and then burned.

Grandpap went to the woods with the grownups every day for a couple of weeks, but finally got bored, and also got tired of being told to stay out of the way all the time.

He decided that he had learned enough about clearing ground to do it all by himself, so one morning after the adults left for the timber, he got a butcher knife from the kitchen and went to the cornfield.

He carefully notched the stalks, finished cutting them from the back side, trimmed off all of the leaves, then ricked the stalks in his own mini log pile. He worked off and on for several days before anyone decided they should check on what he had been doing by himself all that time. Grandpap had managed to clear a significant area, and he was real proud of the job that he had done, until the morning that his dad walked into the clearing.

Grandpap said "Cap, I sure 'nuff got the impression that I shouldn't have cut those cornstalks." He told me that after standing up to eat for the next couple of days he definitely decided to never cut any more corn stalks, unless someone told him that they needed to be cut.

*   *   *   *   *

Grandpap was a great story teller. When I was a little kid, many evenings after supper I would go to the front part of the house, where Grandpap and Grandma lived, and sit next to him in front of the fireplace while he told me stories. One of my all time favorites was about rattlesnakes.

When grandpap was around ten or twelve years old, his parents went to Columbia one morning, and he and Charlie Richardson spent most of the day playing in the creek. They slowly worked their way downstream, wading, skipping rocks, catching frogs, and looking for a hole of water deep enough to swim in.

By the time they finally found some water deep enough to use they were a couple of miles from home, on what used to be the Joe Crane Place. After swimming and laying around for about an hour they decided to go a little further downstream, and inspect a small cave which was located in the bluff by the creek. It wasn't really much of a cave, more like a wide crack in the limestone where a large chunk had slipped out many years before.

When they entered the cave they immediately saw a fairly small rattlesnake, laying next to the wall. They got a couple of stout limbs and clubbed him, then carefully removed four rattles. As they raised up after inspecting him they heard the unmistakable sound of rattlesnake rattles. About 18" above their heads, laying on a ledge, was a large rattlesnake, coiled and ready to strike. Grandpap said that they both fell over backwards and rolled out of the cave, got some rocks and threw at the snake until they knocked him off the ledge, then used the limbs to finish him off.

It was the biggest rattlesnake either of them had ever seen. After removing his twelve rattles the boys decided they had seen all of that little cave they wanted to see, so they got out and headed for home. They made a short detour past a neighbor's house on the way, so they could show off their rattles and brag about killing the snakes. Their neighbor wasn't home, but they talked to his hired hand. After they had told him their story and displayed the rattles, the young man looked at them and said "Yeah, boys, you all are in trouble now. I heard just last week about two boys about your size who killed some rattlesnakes, and while they were pulling the rattles off some of that poison just drifted up and got all over them, and in a couple of weeks all the meat fell off their bones."

Grandpap said they immediately decided it was time to head for home. By the time they got there they were so scared they could hardly talk. Grandpap said his dad always kept a bottle of whiskey in the house, "For medicinal purposes," so they got the whiskey out, poured some in a pan, mixed it with water and carefully washed all of their exposed flesh. When Grandpap reached that point in the story he would always say, almost as an afterthought, "And we might of drank just a little, in case some of the poison had got inside us." He would set there for a few moments puffing on his pipe, then rub his hands together real hard, inspect them carefully, and say "Cap, I guess that whiskey must have worked, 'cause it looks like all the meat is still on my bones."

* * * * *

Grandpap lived 98 years, and he saw more changes during his lifetime than most people can even imagine. He was born during the Civil War, and he lived to see a man in space.

When Grandpap was a young man he cleared ground on the farm with an axe, a cross-cut saw, and a team of mules. He then farmed around the stumps until he had time to grub them out by hand and drag them to a ditch with a team. In later years he stood back and watched as a bulldozer cleared more ground in a day than Grandpap could have cleared in a year.

He went from harvesting grain with a cradle to using a binder and a threshing machine, to then seeing Pappy using a pull-type combine. From cutting hay with a scythe he progressed to riding a mower pulled by a team to then seeing Pappy use a tractor and mounted mower. He went from stacking loose hay to pulling loose hay into the barn loft with a hay-fork and a team, to baling with a mule-powered stationary baler, and finally watching his hay being baled with a self-tying pickup baler.

He cut corn with a corn knife and shocked it, then hauled the shocks to the barn to be shucked out. Sometimes the corn was shucked while it was still standing in the field and thrown into piles on the ground, to be picked up later. From that it went to Pappy using a one-row pull type picker. A couple of years before he died, Grandpap got to see his corn picked and shelled, two rows at a time, as Pappy got Al Britton and Winston Morton to shell his corn with a couple of John Deere 45 Combines with 2 row corn heads.

It Must Be True: Paw-Paw Said So

Grandpap was over 90 years old when this picture was taken.

When Grandpap was a young man he made his trips to town on horseback, or with a team and wagon, and later with a buggy. From that he went to a Model "T" Ford, then to a Model "A" Ford, and finally to modern cars in the 1950s and '60's.

For the last 20 years or so that he was alive Grandpap was perfectly willing for other people to use any kind of new-fangled equipment that came along, but he wasn't the least bit interested in using it himself. He didn't mind things changing, but he figured that he had already changed enough, and he intended to stay just like he was, for however much time he had left.

* * * * *

With a little formal training, Grandpap would have made a hell of a good engineer. He was always designing and building something, and it usually worked. Maybe not at first, but he would revise and remodel until it did.

The cellar on the farm had limestone walls, and when it was dug they must have tapped a wet weather spring, because despite the slope around it, when it rained a lot there would be 6 inches to 2 feet of water in the cellar.

Grandpap broke out some of the cellar floor and put in a piece of 6-inch pipe for a sump and mounted a pitcher spout pump on the floor of the cellar house above. It worked, but it took hours of hand pumping to drain the cellar. After the farm got REA electricity in 1939 Grandpap built a 1 foot wide, 2 feet long and 3 feet tall frame out of 2x2 lumber, and mounted an electric motor on one end. The frame was a mess of shafts, pillow block bearings, right angle gear boxes and various sized pulleys and belts. Grandpap removed the handle from the pump, mounted this frame above it and made the final connection to the pump shaft. He would pour some water down the pump to prime it, flip the switch on the motor, and somehow all those belts and gears finally got power to the pump shaft, and in a couple of hours the cellar would be pumped out.

When we caved in the old cellar house during the 1980s, I salvaged the motor and frame. Chub Gerard bought it, and the last time I saw it, it was in a shed on his farm. I hope it didn't get thrown away.

* * * * *

All of the old horse-drawn machinery on the farm had little additions bolted on in various places that didn't come with the equipment when it was purchased new.

Grandpap was always coming up with something to bolt on machinery to make it work better, or make it easier to use. Most of the additions were worth the time and effort he spent building them. Grandpap had some really good ideas, but it never occurred to him to try to patent any of them, he was just trying to make his work a little easier.

* * * * *

Grandpap and Grandma, 1940's

Grandpap was never one to openly express his feelings. My cousin Prissie said that Grandma told her that one time she asked Grandpap why he never said he loved her. He replied "Well, I told you once, and I still do."

* * * * *

Grandma was in pretty poor health for quite a few years. If she was laying on the bed taking a nap when Grandpap walked in, he would look at her, then ask "Kate, you asleep?" then louder, "Kate, you asleep?" If she still didn't answer he would put his hand on her shoulder and shake her, while asking again "Kate, you asleep?"

Grandma would grump and groan, and finally reply "Not anymore." Thus assured that she was still alive, Grandpap would go on about his business.

Occasionally when I'm dozing in my chair on a Sunday afternoon, Marcia will ask me "Kate, you asleep?"

* * * * *

Whenever a groundhog made a den around the garden or outbuildings, we would haul a barrel of water from the old well by the creek.

Pappy would wait by the backdoor of the den with his shotgun, while Grandpap and I dipped water out of the barrel and poured it into the front hole. After we had dipped enough to lighten the barrel we would tip it over and dump it into the den. One or more groundhogs would rush out of the other entrance to escape the water, and Pappy would greet them with the shotgun. It nearly always worked, and usually Charlie Richardson would come to the farm to get the groundhog carcasses.

* * * * *

Grandpap finished every meal with something sweet. Not just most meals, EVERY meal. At breakfast it was usually a hot buttered biscuit with jelly or syrup, at dinner and supper it could be cake, pie, cookies, pudding, maybe mom's sweet rice, or a bowl of strawberries or sliced peaches with thick cream. He liked it all, but pie was his favorite. Actually, pie crust was his favorite, the filling didn't have to be anything to brag about, as long as the crust was good.

I don't remember Grandpap ever commenting on how good an entire slice of pie was but he was always ready to brag on the crust. I can still hear him today, he would finish his pie, place the silverware on his empty plate, then look at Grandma and say "Good Crust, Kate."

That's kind of a standard saying around our house now. It doesn't matter if it's fried pork chops, broccoli salad, or a pot of beans and country ham, if it's really good, before the meal is over someone is going to look at Marcia and say "Good Crust, Kate." She has come to expect it over the years, and if we don't tell her she's kind of disappointed.

* * * * *

It's a good thing my Grandma never had any contagious diseases when I was a little kid. Anytime I had a spot of dirt on my face (which was most of the time) and I got within grabbing distance of Grandma, her hand would shoot out and she would draw me in. She always wore an apron around the house, and once I was caught she would spit on the corner of her apron and then proceed to scrub as hard as necessary to get the dirt off my face. I never did like having my face washed with warm spit, but it happened lots of times and apparently it didn't hurt me.

* * * * *

When Sis and I were little Grandma always wanted to pick a mess of greens each spring. She was pretty heavy, and walked with a cane, so when we headed for the pasture to pick greens I always carried an old chair for her to set on. She would locate a likely spot and set down, then use her cane to point out what we were supposed to pick.

Grandpap, Grandma, Virginia, Alan and Spot. 1954

By the time we picked a pot full of greens and got back to the house, Grandma was usually so sore and crippled that she had to spend the next 2 or 3 days in bed. But by the next spring she had forgotten how bad it hurt, and she would be ready to go pick another mess of greens.

* * * * *

I was watching "Classic Country" on RFD TV a few weeks ago, when Jeanne Pruitt sang "Jesus Loves Me." It made me think of Grandma. When I was a little kid she used to sing that song to me and Sis. She sat in front of the North door and rocked back and forth in her old chair (which I still have) as she sang. Every time she rocked the chair would chirp.

Jesus Loves Me (chirp) this I know (chirp) for the Bible (chirp) tells me so (chirp). When I was listening to the song on TV, I kept expecting to hear a "chirp" at anytime.

* * * * *

Grandpap farmed in Boone County all his life, except for a couple of years in the early 1900's. Grandpap's brother-in-law ran a grocery store in California for a while, and one spring he convinced Grandpap that running a store in California was better than farming in Missouri, so Grandpap boarded up the house and the whole family got on a train for California, where Grandpap became part owner of a grocery store. After a couple of years he decided he'd rather be home, so he loaded the family on the train again, and they returned to Missouri.

Grandpap never said a whole lot about his time in California, but he did tell me that he got at least one good lesson in merchandising. He said that they had some odd flavored jelly that had been on the shelf for a year without selling, so he told his brother-in-law that they might as well throw it away, but his brother-in-law had an entirely different idea. Grandpap said that they moved the jelly to the front of the store, marked it "special," raised the price a penny a jar, and sold it all the first week. I think that's when Grandpap started thinking about returning to Missouri. He was just too honest for that kind of "creative merchandising."

Grandpap never did have much faith in "specials," and items that were on sale. He said "Watch 'em, Cap, they're trying to get to you."

Grandpap in the California store, 1906. Grandpap is 2nd from right, wearing a vest and necktie.

* * * * *

Grandpap never wasted a whole lot of time explaining things in detail. Once when I was pretty small I asked him where I came from. He said "We found you in a hollow log." End of conversation.

Charlie Richardson

Grandpap and Charlie Richardson pretty much grew up together, and were friends from childhood until Charlie died when he was up in his 80's.

Before the Civil War the Easley family owned Charlie's mother (Mary), and "leased" Charlie's dad (Frank) from his owner. After the war they both stayed and worked for the family for years. When Grandpap's dad died, after being thrown from a horse, Grandpap's mother leased the farm to Frank Richardson, until Grandpap was old enough that he could farm it himself.

Charlie Richardson

I was pretty young when Charlie died and I don't really remember much about him, I just remember that he was out at the farm quite often. He came out and worked until his knees got so bad that he just wasn't able to do it anymore. After that he just came out to visit.

Of course during the 1930s, 40's and 50's, blacks and whites just didn't sit down and eat together. Pappy told me that when he and Charlie would be at the farm alone for some reason, when dinner time came he would set two places at the table, then he and Charlie would set down and eat together. Pappy said that it sure didn't bother him, and that Charlie didn't mind as long as no one else was around.

Pappy told me that one time Grandma baked a pie for them before she left. He said that he didn't feel like fixing dinner that day, so he just cut the pie down the middle and he ate half and Charlie ate half. He said Grandma was a little bit upset, because she had figured on having some pie left for supper. Up until the mid 1970s, some of Charlie's sons and grandsons would come out to the farm occasionally and go rabbit hunting, but I haven't seen any of them in years.

Mr. and Mrs. Charlie Richardson at Grandpap's 80th birthday party, 1944.

Model "T" Fords

Except for Dr. Nifong, Grandpap had the first car in the neighborhood, a 1914 Model T Ford. I still have the original owners manual that came with it.

Pappy said in the winter the roads were so muddy that cars couldn't get around, so Grandpap would disassemble the Model T engine, wrap the parts in oily rags and store them in the house until the next spring. He would then reassemble the engine and be ready for another summer's driving.

When Pappy and Mom got married in 1939 the Model T was still stored in the old garage. Mom said every spring some of the MU engineering class would borrow the car to drive in their parade. Grandpap was tired of fooling around with them every year, so one spring he sold them the car for $10.00. He didn't have to fool around with them anymore, but if the old car was still around it would probably be worth a little more than $10.00.

Model T Ford's didn't have a clutch, they had forward and reverse pedals. When the Model T was replaced with a Model A, Grandpap quit driving, he refused to learn how to operate a clutch. He wouldn't drive a tractor for the same reason, it had a clutch. He also quit shooting when his last hammer gun wore out, he refused to learn how to operate the safety on a hammer-less rifle.

I don't use a computer, and I've never been on-line in my life. I'm afraid if I ever did get on-line I would fall off and get hurt. You don't suppose I inherited some of Grandpap's "stubborn genes," do you?

* * * * *

Model T's had more power in reverse than they did in forward. Pappy told me that when you were driving a Model T you had to back up the really steep hills, because the car would stall out in forward gear.

The road south of the Home Place used to be straight, until people started driving Model T's. Everyone had to back up the hill because they didn't have enough power to get up it going forward. Grandpap traded ground with the County, and they put the sharp curve in the road, to by-pass the worst of the hill. I've wished several times that the curve wasn't there, especially when a damn car misses it and runs through my fence at 2:00 in the morning.

* * * * *

Model T's weren't built to real close specs like today's cars. Pappy said if the main bearings started knocking and you didn't have any money for replacements, you could wrap bacon rind around the crankshaft, bolt everything back together, and drive several hundred miles before you had to replace the rinds. It wasn't a high-tech fix, but it was definitely cheap, and it worked.

* * * * *

When Pappy and Uncle Edward were in their teens they bought a stripped down Model T for $10.00. They drove it all over this part of the county, had it on its side a couple of times, scared a lot of horses, and just generally had a ball with it.

When Uncle Edward got married he didn't think a married man really needed a stripped-down Model T, so they traded it for a portable wood saw with a Witte engine. They sawed wood all over southern Boone County, and made quite a bit of money with it. We sawed wood at home, and for Charlie Hall and Doc Fortney, up until the late 1960s or early '70's. When Pappy finally retired the saw, he sold it to a man from Jefferson City, who planned to restore the engine and saw frame. I've often wondered if he ever got it finished.

Dr. Nifong and "Miss Lavinia"

Pappy and I, and sometimes Virginia, used to fish in Nifong's pond fairly often. We would walk north through the wire gap that went from our chicken yard into the field where Boys and Girls Town is located now, walk about half way to the North end of the field, then turn east into the woods. There was a tractor path through this part of the woods so that we had access for cutting firewood. We would come out on the East side of the woods, turn N.E. across a narrow neck of crop ground, about where the Woodhaven Administration Building is located now, then enter the big woods that ran all the way to the pond. There was somewhat of a tractor path through this part of the woods.

One day as we were walking in this area Pappy said that he wanted to show me something. We turned west off the path for maybe 30 yards, until we came to a white oak tree with the lowest limb cut off about 4 feet out from the trunk. Pappy said that when he and Uncle Edward were kids (around 1910 or 1912) they were playing in the woods and discovered a recently dug hole about 3 feet across and 4 feet deep, directly under the end of that cut off limb.

Pappy said that when they told my Grandpap he said that the stories were that family's that had anything of value buried it during the Civil War, because of all the gorilla activity in Boone County. Nothing was ever heard about who might have buried something there, who came back for it, and whether or not they found what they were looking for, but Pappy said that Grandpap was always convinced that someone was digging for Civil War treasure.

* * * * *

I was visiting with Trent and Vanessa Hall one afternoon when somehow Dr. Nifong became the subject of the conversation. Trent told me that his Aunt Blanch once said "I love Dr. Frank like a brother, but as a Doctor, I wouldn't let him treat my dog."
She probably knew what she was talking about. When Grandma was in her 50's Dr. Nifong operated on her for a hernia. It never healed, and she had a hole in her belly that drained for the next 30 years. She wore a muslin patch taped over it under her clothes.
After her heart problems started, she was in the hospital and Dr. Ladenson was examining her. When he saw the hole he almost exploded before asking "What in the world caused that?" when Grandma told him it was from a 30 year old un-healed hernia surgery he snorted, then scheduled some repair work. When Grandma left the hospital she still had a bad heart, but the hole in her belly was repaired, and well on its way to healing.

* * * * *

Pappy told me that when the gas pipeline was run across the school house field on the Nifong Farm during the 1930s, Dr. Nifong was adamantly opposed to a pipeline on his property. He met with company representatives one time, informed them that there was no way that there would ever be a pipeline installed across his property, and then refused to speak to them again, even going so far as throwing away mail from them, unopened.

The company took the right-of-way by imminent domain, but Dr. Nifong hadn't received any money, because the court hadn't yet determined a price. When the pipe was delivered, company employees cut a gap in Dr. Nifong's fence, and the trucks drove onto the right-of-way and unloaded. After the trucks left Dr. Nifong sent his hired man to the pipe pile with a team of mules and had him drag all the pipe to a nearby ditch and roll it in it.

That was a pretty expensive statement of defiance. The dragging wore the tar paper coating off the pipe, rendering it useless for a buried pipeline. The subsequent court ruling was that the pipe was on Dr. Nifong's farm legally, and he was held liable for damages. Dr. Nifong found out that he wasn't quite as important as he thought he was. He not only got a pipeline across his farm, he had to pay for the pipe it was installed with!

* * * * *

Dr. Nifong's wife, "Miss Lavinia," wasn't nearly as nice a person as she has been portrayed by Nifong Park personnel. She was actually a very bigoted racist, and extremely class conscious. Common people really weren't good enough to associate with her. If common people had to come into her house they came in through the back door, and black people didn't come into her house at all, unless they were employed as servants.

One year when Hazel Wilcox was teaching at Grindstone School, she and her husband Mike rented one of Dr. Nifong's tenant houses. Hazel told mom that when you lived in a Nifong house Miss Lavinia considered you to be her personal servant, on call, at all hours of the day and night. They only lived there for one year.

After the park opened, I took Mom over one Sunday for a tour of the Nifong House. One of the main attractions was Blind Boone's piano. Mom laughed and said if Miss Lavinia knew that all those common people were tracking through her house and looking at her stuff she would turn over in her grave. Then Mom said "and she'd probably climb completely out of her grave if she knew a black man's piano was on display in her house."

* * * * *

Grandpap was one person who was not impressed by Miss Lavinia's money and social status. They had been raised on adjoining farms, they went to grade school together, and Grandpap knew that everything she owned had been given to her. As far as Grandpap was concerned she was Dr. Nifong's wife, no more, no less.

Pappy and Grandpap rented the crop ground on Nifong's farm when I was a kid. When we went to Dr. Nifong's to discuss crop plans we went in the front door, we sat in the living room on the same furniture they sat on, and we ate snacks that were served by Miss Lavinia. Grandpap really didn't care that her parents had been rich, or that she had married a doctor. To him she was still just the spoiled little rich girl he had gone to school with 70 years earlier.

* * * * *

The REA ran electric lines to the area south of Columbia in 1939. Several years before that, Dr. Nifong had a private line run from town out to his farm. I don't know where the line started, but it followed old Highway 63 from Ashland Gravel Road to the farm. It worked pretty good, but tree limbs caused outages from time to time.

Chub Gerard was a lineman for the city, and early one Christmas morning he got a call that Dr. Nifong's power was off. Chub and another lineman left their families on Christmas morning to take care of Dr. Nifong. It took them 2 or 3 hours, but they found the broken line and repaired it, then drove on out to the farm to make sure everything was working.

Chub told me that Miss Lavinia met them at the back door and assured them that everything was working like it should. She then wished them Merry Christmas, gave them each an orange and a dollar bill, and then shut the door. Chub said as far as she was concerned that made everything alright; the common people had served their purpose and been well compensated for their time.

Hog Killing

Does anyone remember how hot the water needs to be to scald a hog? When I was a kid we had a thermometer that we hung in the water in the scalding box, but by the time the water was about hot the thermometer would be so steamed up that you couldn't read it. Pappy or Grandpap would pull off a glove and swipe their finger through the water three times. It needed to be hot enough that they could just barely stand to make the 3rd swipe. Any cooler makes for a slow scald, any hotter and you'll set the hair.

* * * * *

Once when I was 6 or 7 years old, and "helping" on hog killing day, I asked Joe Crane what a "spare rib" was. He said "Well, that one your Grandpap just got done trimming is about as spare as they're ever going to get."

Joe always seemed to have a colored family living in one of his old, shacky tenant houses. The man would always be there to help out at hog killing. He would be set up in the shed between the two smoke houses, and it was always his job to clean the guts. He would start by finding the sweet breads, and then strip out the gut lard for rendering. Most times he would go home with a slab or two of ribs, a liver, and maybe a gallon of lard for his help.

Now Bar-B-Q ribs are a delicacy. Back then they were just something to get rid of. We shaved most of the meat off the ribs and ground it for sausage, then sold the slabs of bones or gave them away. There was too much good meat available after hog killing to waste time gnawing on a damn rib bone.

A couple of times I remember that late in the summer we would have a can of lard left over that had gotten a little rancid. Joe's colored families were always glad to get it. I remember a tall, skinny, grey haired black gentleman named Lewis, who lived in Joe's shack on Rock Quarry Road, telling Pappy that you could boil some potatoes in rancid lard and sweeten it back up. Lewis and his wife had two kids who attended Grindstone School, and rode the same bus that I rode.

We always had enough sweet lard that we never had to try the potato thing, but if you ever get stranded on a mountain with a can of rancid lard that might be a good thing to know.

Hog Killing, 1920

* * * *

When we butchered we always saved the kidneys for one of our city neighbors. We ate mountain oysters (testicles), tongues, brains, liver, sweet breads, hogs head pudding, pickled pigs' feet and cracklings, but we couldn't understand why anyone would want to eat kidneys. Sometime when you see me, ask about the best way to cook kidneys. I have a really good recipe.

Hog Killing, 1940. Still doing it about the same way.

* * * * *

Pappy said the first time he saw someone jack up a car and tie the handle of the sausage grinder to a rear wheel he thought that was the best idea anyone, anywhere, had ever had. I just wish someone would have taken a picture of that operation; I can see it in my mind like it was happening now, but I'd love to have a picture of it.

The sausage mill was mounted on a two-by-twelve board about six feet long. The board would be set on buckets, with someone setting on each end and the handle of the grinder would be fastened to a rear wheel with a long loop of baler twine. I always loved to set on the other end of the board when Pappy was grinding.

Someone would start the car and put it into gear, and then Pappy would start dropping meat into the grinder. He could grind sausage about as fast as they brought meat to him. That setup definitely wouldn't have been OSHA approved, but it sure beat turning that grinder by hand.

*   *   *   *   *

Grandpap loved sausage, and he was always afraid there wouldn't be enough trimmings to make as much as we needed.

When he was trimming hams and shoulders I've seen him pick up a shoulder that was a little smaller than the rest, look at it, then say to me "That's not hardly big enough to cure, Cap, I believe it would make good sausage." He would then cut it into strips and chunks for grinding. When he was done he would look at the pile of meat and say "Cap, that's pretty lean. I believe it needs some more fat in it." Then he would grab some strips of back-fat from the lard pile and add it to the shoulder meat. Then he would say "Cap, take that to your daddy, it will give him something to grind on." Pappy would usually look at a bucket full of this type of meat, shake his head and say "Alan, tell Pap he's getting a little carried away with his sausage meat again." I'd pass on the information, but I don't think it ever made any difference. Grandpap pretty much did what Grandpap wanted to do.

Pork Sausage Seasoning

Edward Everett Easley

To each three gallons of ground meat, take 2/3 cup salt, 1/2 cup black pepper, 1/2 teaspoon Cayenne pepper, and 1 Tablespoon Sage. Mix well. Add to the ground meat and mix thoroughly.

Lots of people sprinkled the seasoning on the meat before grinding. We always mixed it by hand afterwards. We liked to do things the hard way.

* * * * *

One really cold day Joe Crane helped us butcher hogs. When we went to the house for dinner, Joe said "I think I might have froze my finger." He was wearing a glove with a big hole in it, and he had definitely "froze his finger." Grandpap said "Joe, you should have hollered, I've got some extra gloves." Joe replied "Well, I've got 2 new pair out in the car, I was just saving them 'till I needed them worse." That was Joe.

* * * * *

There were always enough older neighbors helping at hog killing that I never got to gut a hog, or block one out. I shot hogs, helped scald them, gamboled them and helped hang them on the pole, then I went and shot another hog.

By the time the last hog was hung there were enough hams, shoulders, sides, etc., laying on the blocking table that I then started carrying meat to the smoke house, for trimming. We had a good 2-wheeled fire wood cart, and the little 4-wheeled wagon that I had as a kid, but it never occurred to anyone to haul meat to the smokehouse, that would have been to easy. The last couple of times that we butchered, when the crew was down to Pappy, Uncle Edward, me and maybe one neighbor, we finally decided to do it the easy way, and we used the cart. I guess when we had plenty of help it didn't really matter.

The smoke houses at the farm, 2012. Still standing.

*   *   *   *   *

It always took 2 days to prepare for hog killing. The scalding box had to be set over a trench, a pile of kindling and old fence posts gathered up for the fire, all of the boards and saw horses for temporary tables had to be hauled from whatever building they were stored in, and given a good washing. Kettles had to be washed and knives sharpened. The lard paddle, squeezers and sausage mill had to be washed, and a good supply of rags placed around in strategic places. We didn't have running water on the farm, so all of the water had to be hand pumped from the cistern, and heated in the big lard kettle in the cellar house.

Pappy said that just once he would like to help butcher at someone else's place. He thought it would be really nice to walk in somewhere, help butcher and then go home, without all of the preparation and cleanup, but it never happened. We always killed our hogs, and however many the neighbors brought in, but I don't remember ever taking a hog to someone else's place to butcher it. And, I don't remember anyone ever helping us get ready to butcher at our place. There was always plenty of help on butchering day, but we always seemed to get everything ready on our own.

Walkup's Station

Carver Walkup in front of his station, early 1950's.

When I was little, Pappy, Virginia and I would go to Walkup's Station every Sunday morning. Pappy would put five gallons of gas in his '37 Chevy, with the price ranging from 14.9 cents to 18.9cents per gallon. Pappy would get a copy of the Sunday "Globe Democrat," then he would get a 5 cent Coke, and Sis and I would get a soda or ice cream bar. If I could talk Pappy out of an extra nickel I would get a bag of salted peanuts to dump into my Pepsi. Walkup's was a great place to catch up on everything that had happened in the neighborhood during the past week, both good and bad.

After Marcia and I got married, and we moved east of town, I would still make a Sunday morning run to Walkup's Station occasionally, just for old times sake.

About the time that Carver sold his station, Tom Singleton opened a service station/grocery store combination on Route WW. It was a lot like Walkup's Station, just not as big, and not quite as wide a variety of activities.

*****

The first time I did anything other than farm work was for Carver Walkup, at his service station, tire store, repair shop, grocery store and occasional auto sales. I might have forgotten something, but that covers most of the things that he did.

The 1st Sunday I helped Carver I got there at 6 am, and Carver and Ruth were gone for the day by 6:30. He knew what he charged for everything so he didn't bother to mark prices. I didn't know what he charged for anything, so it was somewhat of a problem for me. I sold a lot of groceries for whatever the customer wanted to pay. I also left Carver a lot of notes: So and so got 6 cans of beans and a pound of cheese; Joe that works for MU South Farm got a pound of bologna and 2 loaves of bread. I guess Carver got it all figured out, because he never said anything about it, but he did make me a list of most prices before the next Sunday.

I helped Carver off and on for five or six years. The hours were 6:00 am 'till 5:00pm at the earliest, but if I wanted to make 2 or 3 dollars extra, Carver didn't care how late I stayed open.

*****

At that time there was a 2 cent deposit on pop bottles. One day Carver was talking to John King, who ran a liquor store about a quarter mile north of Walkup's. John commented about how many pop bottles three neighbor boys had been turning in for the deposit. Carver said they had been bringing him bottles, too. They started keeping a closer eye on the bottles, and discovered that the boys were stealing bottles from Carver and cashing them in at John King's. Then they would steal bottles from John, and cash them in at Carver's on their way home. They had a pretty good racket going, while it lasted.

* * * * *

Walkup's Station was open from the time I was a little kid until the late 1960s. The guy that bought the station quit doing repair work, quit selling tires, cleaned up all the car parts that were laying around, removed all the loafing stools, raised prices and was out of business in six months. The customers liked it the way it was when Carver owned it.

Growing Up in the 1950s

Before we had a power lawn mower most of the yard just grew up until hay season, when Pappy would mow it with the tractor. However, Grandpap had a push type reel mower, and he kept a section mowed east and south of the house. When he would start mowing I would get Virginia's doll buggy and walk beside him every round, pushing the buggy and "helping Grandpap mow."

* * * * *

When Sis and I, Tom and Jim Watson and Kenny and John Cavcey walked back and forth to school (barefoot, in the snow, uphill both ways) we were pretty easily entertained. People drank beer back then, and threw their empty cans into the road ditch, just like they do now. The cans were all steel, some of them with a cone-shaped top and pop bottle type cap. We would hunt the road ditch for cans, then stomp our heels into the center of the cans, causing them to clamp tightly on our shoes. We would then walk to or from school, with the cans going clank, clank, clank as we walked down the gravel road.

We also watched for blackberries, wild grapes, or anything else edible we could find. We would also pull horseweeds or milkweeds and push them down the road, pretending they were cars. A real good one would make two or three trips.

Once, when our first grandson, Justin, was about three years old, he was with me when I was cutting wheat. We had moved the combine to a new field about a half mile down the road, and were walking back to get the truck, Justin remarked that it sure was a long way to walk, and I wasn't about to carry him, so I pulled a big weed and told him how I used to push weeds and pretend I was driving a car.

He pushed it a little ways, then raised one arm over his head, holding the weed horizontally. I asked him what he was doing, and he replied that cars were o.k., but he'd rather fly a helicopter. At least it made that half mile walk get a lot shorter for him.

*   *   *   *   *

When I was a kid lots of homes in our neighborhood were still heated with wood or coal, and the rest had oil burning stoves or furnaces. People were starting to cook with L.P. Gas, but Charlie and Beulah Hall still cooked with wood up until they sold their farm to Rock Bridge Park and moved to town in the early 1960s

I can just barely remember when we got the first gas cook stove at the farm. There were two 100# L.P. bottles set next to the outside kitchen wall and when one bottle was used up the valve was switched to the full bottle, and a phone call was made to Pauley's Store in Ashland for a replacement. For the price of the gas only, no delivery charge, the store would make the 30 mile roundtrip, hook up a full bottle and take the empty to be refilled. I don't suppose there is an L.P. dealer anywhere in Boone County today who would deliver one 100# bottle of L.P. for free. When you consider the price of gas and diesel there's really not much way that they could afford to do it now.

Sis and I, and Kenny and John Cavcey, were told regularly that those two gas bottles were dangerous, and we were not to mess around them. Dangerous didn't really agree with us, so we pretty much kept our distance. One day not long after a new bottle had been delivered, we were playing in the sand box, which was about 75 feet from the bottles. Apparently the new bottle had been over filled, and after a couple of hours in the sun the pop-off valve went off and a cloud of gas erupted with an extremely loud hissing noise.

John Cavcey, Virginia Easley, Kenny Cavcey and me, mid 1940's. Grandpap built the 2-wheeled cart for me, and I wore it completely out before Santa brought me a 4-wheeled wagon.

That sounded plenty dangerous to us, so we partially climbed, partially jumped and partially fell over the gate to the wood lot, and didn't stop running until we reached the hog house at the South end of the lot. By the time we got there the eruption was over, and Mom and Grandma had come rushing out of the house to see what was going on. Mom went back inside and called Pauley's, while Grandma started trying to coax us back to the yard. It took her a while to get us there. It didn't smell real good down by the hog house, but it sure seemed a lot safer to four little kids who had been pretty much brainwashed about those "dangerous" gas bottles.

* * * * *

Raymond Hendricks had the 1st contract to furnish transportation in the New Haven School District. He started hauling kids to the one room schools several years before the New Haven building was built. Raymond drove himself, plus other drivers I remember are Jimmy Phillips, Arno Winkler, Dysart Barnes and C. W. Sapp. There were many others over the years that I don't recall.

Raymond's 1st bus was a 1949 Chevy Panel truck. He later added a 1952 Ford Panel truck, and a '52 Ford with a 24 passenger school bus body.

The seats in the panel trucks were 2X12 boards mounted on brackets along each side. The double doors in the back of the panel were the emergency exit. After a little use, those 2/12s became polished and slick. The kids riding on the driver's side had the driver's seat to slide into, but there was nothing on the other side, so the biggest kid on the bus rode in front and braced his feet during stops, to keep everyone from sliding off.

My freshman year in high school I was the 1st one on the bus in the morning, getting on at 6:30 A.M. In the afternoons Raymond ran the route backwards, so I was the last one off. I rode that bus 120 miles a day, to make a 16 mile round trip, but it still beat walking. I'm glad it was then, not now. I don't think my butt would last for 120 miles on a 2X12, in the back of a panel truck.

*   *   *   *   *

When I was a kid there were some big Catalpa trees in the yard at the farm. As a matter of fact, they're still there today. In hot weather, before going to the field, Pappy and Grandpap would pick several large Catalpa leaves and put them in the top of their straw hats. They even got Tom and Jim Watson and I to use the leaves. Grandpap also carried a couple of rags in his pocket, and if there weren't any good leaves available he would dip a rag in the creek, and put a wet rag in his hat.

It works better with a straw hat than it does with a seed corn cap because there is more air circulation, but it helps with either one. It works on the same principle as the evaporator on an air conditioner, but most people look at you like you're crazy if you tell them about putting tree leaves in your hat.

*   *   *   *   *

There basically wasn't any traffic when I was growing up. Pappy taught me to drive the old "37 Chevy when I was 9 years old, and as long as I stayed on the gravel, I pretty much got to drive whenever I wanted to.

I took my driving test just a day or 2 after I turned 16. When I finished my test the Highway Patrolman asked me how long I had been driving. When I said since I was 9 years old he replied "that figures. You've had plenty of time to pick up several bad habits." I passed the test, but he didn't think I could drive nearly as good as I thought I could.

* * * * *

John Cavcey and I used to roam the whole country side. We weren't old enough to carry guns and hunt by ourselves, so we just roamed. The old abandoned house on the Limerick Place had an outside stairway to the attic. The attic door was pad locked, but we could take our pocket knives and pry out the nails that held the hasp, and get into the attic. The only thing there was a bunch of old musty law books, from when Harry was in school, but we'd check it out occasionally anyhow, just because we knew we shouldn't.

* * * * *

One year Hale Cavcey made a crock full of grape wine. After it was pretty well ready, Kenny and John stashed a tin cup in the garage over the cellar, and we would slip into the cellar with the cup, and sample Hale's wine.

I don't know if he ever figured out why so much of the wine "evaporated," but there sure wasn't much left for him to bottle.

* * * * *

When I was growing up, Pappy and Grandpap had an old Case combine that just wouldn't run for more than 2 or 3 days in a row without needing some type of repair. At that time the nearest Case dealer was in Jefferson City.

Whenever the old combine broke down Pappy would get his billfold and car keys, then Grandpap and I would get in the car with him and we'd head for Jeff City. It didn't matter how big of a hurry we were in, when we went through Ashland we always stopped at Uncle Charles and Aunt Sara's house for a short visit.

One day when we pulled into their driveway and got out of the car, Prissie (my cousin) came to greet us. She had been out in the yard, sun bathing. That was before the time of bikinis', but she was wearing shorts and a halter-top. I was probably 12 years old at the time, and Prissie was in high school. I took a good long look at her, and that was the first time that I thought just maybe there might be something to this boy/girl stuff after all.

Sorry, Pris, but I just had to tell that.

* * * * *

On Sunday afternoons, if we didn't have a neighborhood baseball game going on, John Cavcey, Leroy Dirksmeyer and I would walk 6 or 7 miles to town, go to a movie and then walk home. I wouldn't walk 100 yards to go to a movie now.

Leroy Dirksmeyer and Me, 1956.

Leroy was the first one of the bunch to get a car, a 1948 Chevy business coupe. Three people could ride in the seat, and two more could skrunch up with some pillows on the wide shelf behind the seat, where brief cases and salesmen's samples were supposed to go. It wasn't very comfortable, but it sure beat walking.

After Greg and Jeff (our sons), got too old for a swing set, we sold ours to Leroy and his wife Marilyn. A few years later Leroy committed suicide. John moved to the state of Washington after he got out of high school. He's been back maybe a half dozen times over the years.

* * * * *

Once after I had smacked the front of Pappy's '51 Chevy pretty hard, our discussion finally reached the point of when Pappy and Uncle Edward were young.

Pappy said that they were returning from town one Saturday night, and as they turned off of what is now Old Highway 63 onto what is now Grindstone Parkway they were going way to fast and the buggy wound up on its side, with the shafts broken out. The team was o.k., and Pappy and Uncle Edward were alright except for a few scrapes and bruises, but Pappy said Grandpap was not real happy with them.

I asked Pappy several times if they had been partying a little too hard that night, but the only answer I ever got was that little smile of Pappy's.

* * * * *

After attending the one room Grindstone School for eight years, and then Freshman year at U-High, which was really a pretty small school, I transferred to Hickman High so that I could be in FFA (Future Farmers of America).

The first morning after I got off the school bus and walked into the lobby at Hickman I looked around and thought "My God, what in the hell am I doing here?" I had never seen so many kids in one place in all of my life, and most of them seemed to know each other. Except for the ones who had gotten off of the bus with me I didn't see anyone that I knew.

I made it through my first five classes in sort of a daze, and finally walked into Mrs. Keller's sixth period World History class. I looked around to see if I knew anyone there and the first person that I noticed was this really pretty dark haired girl sitting in the third row. She flashed me a smile that reached from ear to ear and patted the empty desk next to her. As soon as I sat down she stuck out her hand and said "Hi, I'm Joanie Puckett." It was the first smile or friendly word that I'd had all day. We pretty much talked through the whole class, despite several admonishments from Mrs. Keller. As a matter of fact we pretty much talked through the whole year, despite MANY admonishments from Mrs. Keller.

I sure wouldn't say that my three years at Hickman were the most enjoyable three years of my life, but I made it through them. Joan and I always seemed to have at least one class together each year, and I always considered her one of my best friends. The last time that Marcia and I saw Joanie and Phil was at our 50th High School Reunion in 2010. About three weeks after Marcia died I got a card from them, they had just heard about my baby. When I saw what Joanie had written I broke down and cried again. Passing years and 2000 miles didn't seem to make much difference, good friends are there forever.

* * * * *

When I turned sixteen years old I had some money saved up from hauling hay and working for neighbors, and the only thing I could think of to spend it on was a car. Pappy told me "Boy, don't waste your money on a piece of junk, wait 'til you have enough to get something decent." I didn't think that I could save enough in another week to make much difference, and I wanted a car NOW.

Most of my friends had '49-'51 Fords, some of them in real good condition. I knew that I couldn't afford a nicer car than most of them had, so I decided I would own an uglier car. I couldn't find an old Hudson so I did the next best thing, I bought a '51 Mercury. It wasn't as ugly as a Hudson, but it was almost the ugliest car I had ever seen. It would have been a pretty fair old car if it had been treated right, but it sure didn't get much decent treatment from me. One big problem it had was a weak accelerator spring. It seemed every time I got in the car the accelerator went to the floor and stayed there until I got where I was going. The old Mercury was

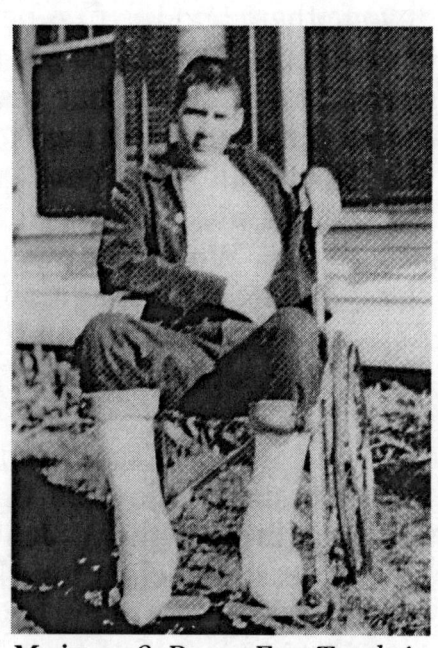

Me in 1958. Damn Fast Trucks! Elra Sapp, Billy Butzin, and Billy Strawn pretty much destroyed this wheelchair during the 3 months they pushed me around in it.

pretty heavy, and the combined weight of the car and my foot was just more that the transmission could stand. The first six months I had the car I put three junk yard transmissions in it.

One Saturday morning my car had been setting for several days, waiting for another transmission, so I borrowed Pappy's Chevy to go to the junk yard and look for one. I didn't quite get there. About a mile from home, where the gravel road met Highway 63, I put a little too much strain on the old Chevy. As I pulled onto the pavement, with the wheels churning in the gravel, the rear axle snapped and I coasted to a stop. I walked up the road to Walkup's Station and Buddy Fleetwood and Charlie Gibson came back with me, and we pushed the car to the station.

I couldn't find anyone heading my way, so I slowly walked back home. I knew what would happen when I got there, so the closer I got the slower I walked. When I turned in the driveway Pappy and Mom were setting in the yard, and as I walked up to them Pappy looked at me and asked what happened. When I told him he looked at me again, then shook his head and said; "GOOD GOSH-A-MIGHTY, ALAN!"

I spent every evening the next week looking for parts and repairing cars. It took two more transmissions before I started easing up on that poor old Mercury, but I finally figured out that there were better ways to spend my time and my money than installing transmissions in old junk cars.

* * * * *

The morning that Marcia died there were thirteen family members, plus our preacher Dennis Swearngin, crowded into her room at the Hospital. At some point my Daughter-in-law, Jamie, said "Paw-paw, I know you and Marcia dated in high school, how did you meet her?"

I replied that I was standing in front of the VO-AG building with some of my friends, when one of them said "Alan, you see that girl over there? One of her friends told me that if you would ask her out she'd probably go." With that incentive I took another good look, then said "Oh hell yes!" Someone in the room, I think it was Leah, asked how long after that it was before I asked her out. I answered, "How long does it take to walk across the parking lot at Hickman High School?"

Marcia Wilkerson, Summer 1959, three months after we met. Oh Hell Yes!

I'll never forget that morning. She looked like she was about 6 feet tall, as big around as a broom handle, and she was wearing a red dress with white flowers on it that quit about 6 inches above her knees. Among other things, I thought to myself "My, my my my!" Whatever it was, it sure worked good for 52 years and it's still working. God, Baby, I miss you so much!

* * * * *

One beautiful spring morning when I was a junior in high school, Billy Butzin and I decided that it was just too nice of a day to attend school, or at least too nice of a day to attend our school.

Just before time for class to start we walked out to the parking lot, got in my ugly old Mercury, and headed for Centralia. When we got to the Centralia High School we waited until a break between classes, then went in the school and looked around until we found one of our FFA (Future Farmers of America) friends. When he asked us what we were doing in Centralia we told him that we were taking an unguided tour.

We coached him a little on what to say, then we went to class with him. He introduced us to the teacher, then told her we were doing research on teaching methods in various high schools for our civics class. She seemed to accept the story, and we were properly attentive as we observed her teaching methods, asked her an occasional question, and took notes in some hastily borrowed notebooks.

We attended three more classes with our friend, gave the same story each time, and were never questioned. However, by that time nearly everyone in the school knew what was going on, and there was a lot of talk about it, and we started to get some questioning looks from some of the teachers as we walked in the halls between classes. We decided that we were probably pushing our luck, so we quietly slipped out to the parking lot and headed back to Columbia, feeling very proud of ourselves for pulling off such a wonderful scam.

While we were on our way home, laughing about what we had done, some of the Centralia teachers got their heads together and decided that something about this whole affair just didn't seem right, so they made a phone call to our school which effectively neutralized any excuses we might have thought up to explain our absence.

The weather was beautiful for the next two weeks, and Billy and I got to observe it through the window of the principal's office for two hours each day after school, as we paid the price for our "unguided tour."

*   *   *   *   *

The following year, we had one of the worst late March snow storms Boone County had experienced for many years. When school let out for the day the wind was blowing, it was snowing so hard that it was almost impossible to see, and there was already four or five inches of snow on the ground.

I had just traded my ugly old Mercury off for a '55 Chevy two door hardtop, and I wasn't about to head for the country in my new car, so I went to the pool hall until 5:00 p.m., then drove to my Aunt Pauline and Uncle Edward's house and told them I needed to spend the night with them, since I didn't think I could make it home. We always had a lot of fun together, and since I hadn't seen them for a couple of months we had a very enjoyable evening.

The next morning Aunt Pauline fixed a big breakfast, then she left for work with Uncle Edward while I waited until time to leave for school. I had the radio on, and I soon heard a list of cancellations. Hickman High School was open, but it was announced that none of the buses were running out in the country. I decided that if there were no buses running no one would expect me to be at school, so I loafed around the house until noon, then went to the pool hall.

I called home around 4:00 p.m., and Pappy told me the roads were still drifted shut, so I went back to my Aunt and Uncle's for another night. The next morning the buses still weren't running, so I went back to the pool hall.

I really enjoyed shooting pool when I was in high school, but by 5:00 p.m. on the second day the fun was beginning to wear thin, and I was hoping that the buses would run the next day, so I would have a reason to go back to school. The next morning it was announced that all the buses were running again, so I thanked Aunt Pauline and Uncle Edward for their hospitality, then headed for school. When I walked into the office to get my absence slip the principal looked at me and asked where I had been for the past two days. I replied that the roads were drifted shut and the buses hadn't been running. He said "I know that, but you were in town, why didn't you come to school?" It seems that a teacher on lunch break had seen me entering the pool hall, and had dutifully reported that to him when she returned to school.

Our principal, old Chevy, never did have any sense of humor, and none of my arguments made much of an impression on him, so the next week I once again had the privilege of spending two hours each day in the office after school. When I got home and tried to explain to Pappy why I wouldn't be home from school in time to do my chores the next week, he sat there for a few moments, shook his head, then once again shared his favorite expression with me; "GOOD-GOSH-A-MIGHTY, ALAN!"

* * * * *

It's November, 2012, and The Hostess Bakery, makers of "Twinkies," is closing permanently after filing for Bankruptcy.

When I attended Grindstone School in the late 1940s and early '50's, recess was usually fairly unstructured. Some of the kids played on the swings and teeter-totters, while others might play ball, Annie-over, stink-base (prisoner's tag) or whatever else we thought of, while the teacher spent most of her time inside grading papers.

Grindstone School was at the corner of Old Highway 63 south and Grindstone Road. At that time Old 63 was still the main north/south route through the state, and Grindstone was just a little narrow county gravel road. There was a woven wire fence with two barbs on top around the school yard, with a wooden farm gate at the entrance and a stile-block over the West fence so we could retrieve baseballs and footballs from Ed Wilson's pasture without stomping down the fence.

One day at recess a panel truck with a Hostess Bakery logo on the side stopped at the edge of the highway. The driver got out and asked one of the older kids if he could talk to our teacher. When she came out he told her that with her permission he would like to give everyone there a Hostess snack. She agreed, and he passed out Twinkies to the teacher and all of the kids.

That was the first time I had ever eaten a Twinkie. They never were my favorite snack, but that free sample sure tasted good at the time.

* * * * *

My sister, Virginia, says there is a tradition that the Easley and Cheavens men were alcohol free, but mostly it is a myth, perpetuated by wives and mothers who think that the men should be alcohol free.

I especially remember one cold day at the farm when I was young. We had butchered hogs, it was getting late, and things were pretty much done for the day. Everyone was in the cellar house by the stove, where Pappy was cooking off a kettle of lard, when Chub Armstrong showed up to buy some ribs. He walked into the cellar house and greeted everyone, then pulled a pint of whiskey out of his pocket, took a drink and then passed it around. By the time the bottle got back to him it was empty, so he recapped it and tossed it into the trash. I didn't notice anyone refuse a drink as the bottle went by, so there goes that alcohol free myth.

Also, when we used to saw wood for Doc Fortney, after we finished Doc would bring out a bottle of homemade wine and some glasses. Kenny and John Cavcey and I never got any, but I don't think anyone else missed out. There goes that alcohol free myth again.

When Sis and I were little, there was never any whiskey in the house, except at Christmas time. Pappy told me once that anything that tasted as good as whiskey shouldn't be kept where it's easy to get to. There goes that alcohol free myth again, I think it's just about completely gone.

Pappy and Momma

Pappy and Mom, July 1973.

When I started this section called "Pappy and Momma," I really thought there would be a lot more stories in it. However, nearly every time I wrote something that featured Pappy or Mom, I realized that it would fit really nice under some other category, so this section is pretty thin. There is a lot of Pappy and Momma in the book, but it's pretty much scattered throughout the whole thing.

A year or two before Pappy died I was helping him fix fence one morning. After a couple of hours he sat down and said "Alan, I appreciate the help, but I can get more done without you. You've worn me out already, I'm done for the day. When I work by myself and go at my own pace, I can work all day." Now, I know what he meant. Greg can wear me slick in about an hour.

Pappy and Mom fixing fence, November 1981. This picture was taken 3 months before Pappy died.

* * * * *

Pappy was born on the farm south of Columbia where I was raised, and Momma was born and raised in New York City, in an apartment house that was managed by her dad. It was located two blocks from ground zero, where the World Trade Centers were destroyed.

Somehow Pappy's sister, Aunt Mary, wound up living and working in New York City. She and Mom became friends, and one spring Aunt Mary asked Mom if she wanted to spend her vacation on a farm in Missouri. Mom thought that sounded like fun, so a few weeks later she wound up at the farm with Aunt Mary.

Pappy said that the first time he saw Mom he thought she was the "spiffiest looking little thing" he had ever seen. It was hay season and Pappy was in the field all day, every day, and Aunt Mary and Mom were visiting Aunt Mary's friends at night so all Pappy and

Mom did for a week was make eyes at each other during dinner and supper. On Saturday night, before she was leaving for New York on Sunday, they went to a movie.

Mom said that after the movie they went to a diner and were setting at a table drinking coffee, when Pappy suddenly said "Pap's too old to run the farm by himself we'll have to live with them." Mom said she thought about it for just a moment, then told him "that's fine." She said that was as close as Pappy ever came to a proposal.

Three months later Pappy headed for New York in a Model "A" Ford. Their plans were to return to the farm to get married, but Pappy told me that by the time they got to Alexandria, Virginia, they decided they had better find a preacher. Pappy got a phone book and started calling Baptist preachers, and the first one that answered, they went to his house and got married.

Pappy was 40 years old and had never lived away from the farm, and Mom was 30 years old and had lived in New York all of her life. They were the only two people in the world who thought it would last. Mom said that her Boss told her when she left that he would hold her job for her for a year, and she was welcome back anytime she was ready to come. Pappy said if he'd had enough money to cover all the bets he was

Pappy and Mom, August 1940.

offered, he would have been a rich man, because no-one gave them a year. They fooled a lot of people, they had been married 42 years, when Pappy died in 1982.

* * * * *

I don't think that I ever heard Pappy say a cuss word until my 12th birthday. Then I found out that he knew ALL of them. Pappy and Grandpap were in the Nifong field just north of our house combining wheat, and I was across the road at Cavcey's, messing around in the yard with John. Pappy's all time favorite dog, Pudge, was with me.

A concrete truck came down the road at a pretty fast clip, with the chute rattling, dust fogging and gravel flying. Pudge ran to the road to challenge this monster, slipped, and went under the rear wheels. The truck never even slowed down. John helped me carry Pudge home, then he went back to his house while I went to the field to tell Pappy and Grandpap what had happened.

Pappy said "He didn't stop? That no good son-of-a-bitch!" He headed

Pappy and Pudge, 1954.

for the house, with Grandpap and I following. Pappy got his car keys, then we walked to the garage, climbed in the car, and headed down the road. At Channing Crane's place we saw the truck, backed up to the garage with the chute still down. Pappy pulled up in front of the truck and we got out. The driver walked over and asked it he could help us. He was probably 6'4" tall, weighed around 275 pounds, and was dressed in bib overalls with no shirt. Pappy was 5'4" tall, and might have weighed 130 pounds at the time.

Pappy asked "Did you just come down the road in that truck?" When the driver said that he had, Pappy looked up at him and said "You no good son-of-a-bitch, you ran over this boys dog, on his birthday, and you didn't even have the decency to stop." The guy tried to explain that he didn't know he had hit a dog, but Pappy wasn't in any mood to listen.

Pappy stood there about a foot from the driver looking up at him, and gave him the most thorough cussing I have ever heard anyone get. The guy's mouth dropped open and he stood there looking down at Pappy with an "I can't believe this is happening" look on his face. Pappy used all of the available words, and when he finally started through them again Grandpap reached out and took hold of his elbow and said "That's enough, William, you've made your point."

When we got home Mom and Grandma wanted to know if we had found the truck. I said yes, and started to tell them what had happened. Grandpap gave me a sharp look and said "He didn't know he hit the dog, we got it worked out." We buried Pudge under the grapevines, and though we talked about Pudge quite a bit for a while, I don't recall that the cussing incident was ever mentioned again.

* * * * *

Several years after Pappy died, Mom repeatedly heard squeals, growls and loud thumps in her attic. She kept asking me what I could do about it. Not wanting to get her hopes too high, I told her "Don't worry about it, I'll get 'em when I have time." Knowing me like she did, she replied that she hoped whatever it was wouldn't smell too bad when they died of old age.

One morning just before 5 a.m. my phone rang and Mom said "I'm sorry to wake you, but I couldn't wait any longer. There are three coons in my bedroom." It seems that modern technology didn't take into consideration the fact that three full grown coons are heavy enough to override the springs on a fold down attic staircase. Marcia and I immediately drove to Mom's to see what could be done. Actually, to see what had already been done.

Three coons in the bedroom for three hours equals utter devastation. The window curtains were ripped from the curtain rods, the control knobs were off the air conditioner, pictures and whatnots were on the floor, mom's sewing basket was overturned and the contents scattered, and one corner of the room had been turned into a latrine that looked like all the coons in Boone County had been using it.

I couldn't find the old hog catcher that Pappy used to have, so I got the bright idea that I would drive them out with a broom. Sure! If you think hogs or chickens are hard to drive, you ought to try driving coons. One went back up the staircase, but the other two wouldn't even get close to it. I shut the stairs and tried driving the others into the kitchen then out the back door. The two that were left were apparently blind, because they sure couldn't see the door. Three times around the bedroom was enough to get them pretty upset, so I left them under the bed while I drank some coffee and did some further planning.

Got it! I'd lasso them! Good idea, but it was just like trying to lasso a round ball of fur. The first time I threw the rope and missed they sat down and tucked their heads between their front legs and ignored me. I gave up on the lasso and chased them with the broom until they got mad again, then I drank some more coffee.

I decided that I probably needed some advise, so I called the fire department. They said shoot them. Nope, not in the bedroom. It was messy enough already, besides that, I had already shot a hole in the barn roof several years before, and I wasn't about to take a chance on shooting a hole in the bedroom floor. Then they suggested driving them out, but I already knew that wouldn't work. Their last suggestion was call a Missouri Conservation agent. I liked that idea and tried it, but got no answer.

I thought maybe more warm bodies would help so I called Greg and Jeff, then drank more coffee until they got there. It seemed like three grown men, plus Marcia and Mom, should be able to drive two little coons out of the house. We chased them until we got them mad again, then we drank more coffee.

Finally, Greg devised a make-shift hog catcher, using a broom handle and some heavy twine. We caught them one at a time and drug them squalling through the kitchen and out the back door. We were so glad to get them out that we forgot to shoot them, we just turned them loose.

We nailed the staircase shut before we left and it was probably a good thing. By that night, they were back in the attic. Since then on two separate occasions coons have fallen through the plaster ceiling into the living room, but we now keep a hog catcher on hand and have the routine down pat. It takes a lot longer to fix the ceiling that it does to remove the coon.

Mom had coons in the attic until she died, and groundhogs under the house. Now, Jeff has the pleasure of putting up with them. I keep expecting the groundhogs to break through the floor so that they can join in the fun.

* * * * *

Pappy never did a lot of mushroom hunting, but he usually found at least one mess every spring. The easiest ones that he found were in the North yard, under one of the big catalpa trees. Every 2nd or 3rd year enough would come up there to make Pappy and Mom a good meal. The driveway has gotten wider over the years, and the mushroom patch is now covered with gravel.

One spring after Pappy died the mushrooms came up a little late, and grass had outgrown them. Greg mowed Mom's yard one afternoon, and I stopped by a couple of hours later to visit her. As I walked across the yard I spotted what looked like part of a mushroom. I got down on my hands and knees, sorted through the short grass and clippings, and came up with enough mowed mushroom pieces to make Mom a meal. She said that mowing didn't hurt their flavor at all, but that it was kind of hard to get all the grass clippings off them before cooking.

* * * * *

Mom always had beautiful flowers. She had beds of daffodils, tulips, iris and holly hocks, plus all of the little gibberish stuff that has to be planted every spring. As the years went by she spent less and less time working with her flowers, until finally all that was left was some iris and daffodils that made it on their own.

One day when she was in her early 90's she was at our house, and she went outside with Marcia to look at the flowers. She said "Marcia, there're beautiful, but I can't imagine anyone doing this much work to raise flowers." I reminded her that she used to do the same thing, and she replied that it didn't seem like that much work back then.

Marcia

Now, where Marcia's flower beds used to be a few tough old iris and daffodils come up each spring, but the little stuff's about gone. There seems to be a direct correlation between age and energy level. I wonder why that is?

* * * * *

I'd hate to accuse my sweet little momma of being hardheaded, but if she wasn't she was sure borderline.

Before Aunt Mary died she and Mom talked on the phone every day. The first week after Aunt Mary's funeral Mom told me she hadn't talked to anyone all week, so I convinced her to get one of those Medic-Alert buttons to wear around her neck, just in case something happened.

Well, something finally happened, one hot July afternoon Mom had a mild stroke. She was out in the yard and she passed out. When she woke up she couldn't get up, so did she push the button? Hell, no!

She spent well over an hour, scooting backwards a little at a time until she finally reached the house, and by holding on to the door she was able to regain her feet.

I called Mom every evening after supper to check on her, and that night when she told me what had happened I asked her why in the world she didn't push the button. She very indignantly replied, "Alan, I did not feel good. The last thing I wanted was a lot of lights and sirens, and a bunch of people I didn't even know running around my yard messing with me."

She never did use that button, but she still had it around her neck when she finally had to go to a nursing home at the age of 96.

* * * * *

After Pappy passed away in 1982 Momma lived by herself on the farm for the next 23 years, before finally going to a Nursing Home for a year. She enjoyed life up until the last few months, but eventually she said "Enough is Enough! this is lasting a year too long." She told me to never get real old. She said "Get really close, then fall over on your face, dead."

Pappy and Mom with their Grandsons, Karl and John DeMarce, and one of the last big woodpiles. October 1972.

Mom was pretty strong willed, and she did pretty much as she pleased, and if someone didn't like it that was their problem, not hers. Once at the Nursing Home she was commenting on how fat some of the help was. She spread her hands as far apart as she could reach and said "I don't think you can work here unless your bottom is this wide." I told her not to talk so loud, that someone might hear her. She replied "I'm 97 years old and I'll say anything I want to say, who's going to stop me?" That was my Momma.

Guns and Hunting, and Fishing Too

Pappy, Uncle Edward, Guy Judd, Robert Ricks, Carl Holloway and others spent lots of long nights coon hunting during the late teens, 1920s and '30's.

At the time wages were 50 cents per day, and Pappy said a good coon skin would bring $5.00, so it was definitely worth their time. Of course coons weren't nearly as plentiful then as they are now. Pappy said he could hunt all season, with some really good hounds, and 5 or 6 coons was a good year. Now you can run over that many with your pickup in a year.

Pappy said they always carried some salt when they were coon hunting. He said that he never really cared for raw eggs, but at 2 or 3 o'clock in the morning, a couple of raw eggs, "Borrowed" from some ones hen house, would slide down pretty good with a little salt on them, and help fill an empty spot until they could get home for breakfast.

* * * * *

When I was growing up, Pappy had a .22 Remington pump that he had purchased new in 1919. It was completely shot out. The last time we took it hunting, we took turns shooting at a squirrel until finally one of us got lucky and hit him.

The next time Pappy was in town, he went to Western Auto and bought a new Remington pump. It was bigger and heavier than the old rifle, and Pappy never liked it as well. E. J. Kelly rebuilt the old gun for me several years ago, and it's in better shape now than the "new" gun. I don't shoot either one of them anymore, I just like having them around.

I also have Pappy's 12 gauge double barrel LeFever. I still shoot it occasionally, just to remind myself how hard it kicks. I killed my first rabbit with that LeFever, and I love the old gun, but it can knock you on your butt. Just ask my Grandson, Clint.

* * * * *

As soon as I was big enough to follow, Pappy started taking me hunting. We wouldn't go far, I was too little to go very far. We'd just slip into Nifong's woods far enough to kill a squirrel, then we'd head for home. The bigger I got, the farther we'd go, but by the time I got big enough for a really long hunt Pappy was starting to slow down, and he didn't want to go too far.

In later years he pretty much contented himself with fishing, since it required a lot less walking. Pappy and Uncle Edward really enjoyed each others' company, and they spent a lot of time together, fishing.

Stephen, Clint, and Greg with supper.

* * * * *

Greg and Justin with Justin's first deer, November 2000.

When I was a kid lots of the neighbor boys had BB guns. I wanted one so bad I couldn't hardly stand it, but Pappy said "NO." He felt that when I was old enough for a gun I would be old enough for a real gun. He thought that BB guns were only good to get kids hurt or in trouble. A few days before my 12th birthday we were in town, and Pappy said "Let's go by the Western Auto Store and see what they have in the way of .22 rifles." They had a nice Remington single-shot bolt-action, Pappy bought it for me, and I still have it today.

A few days after my birthday, I asked Pappy if I could go hunting and he nodded and said "Just remember what I've taught you and you'll be fine." I tried to pass some of that knowledge along to Greg and Jeff when they got old enough to hunt alone, and apparently it worked. Greg does a lot of hunting, and Jeff hunted until he hurt his back. They passed it on down to their kids, and hopefully there will be several more generations of Easley's who enjoy guns and hunting.

* * * * *

Charlie Hall was always willing to let people hunt and fish on his property. There were always a few people who slipped in without asking, and he didn't really like that, but I don't know of anyone that he told no, if they came to him and asked permission. Pappy, Virginia and I used to fish on Charlie a lot, usually in the Mill Dam hole, but I don't remember that Pappy and I ever hunted on Charlie. When we hunted it was either at home or at Dr. Nifong's.

After Marcia and I got married we lived for a while in the little house on Wat Cheavens' place below Pierpont. Marcia had to work until noon on Saturdays, so I would have her let me out along the road somewhere, I would hunt my way to Pappy's and Mom's, and she would pick me up on her way home.

There were nothing but Fox Squirrels at Pappy's, but just a couple of miles south at Charlie's place there were lots of grey squirrels. I'd always squirrel hunted with a .22 rifle, but after watching grey's run on the ground or through the tree tops at a high rate of speed, and not even getting a shot I decided that a shotgun was the way to go, so I bought a brand new Stephens 16 gauge double barrel Model 311A, for $62.50 from Chub Armstrong at Tee Pee Town.

Greg Easley and squirrels, January 1, 1975

With the shotgun I started getting as many greys as I did Fox squirrels. I loved that little Stephens from the minute Chub showed it to me, and I still love it today.

Over the years I bought Greg and Jeff each one like it, and I found a 12 gauge 311A for myself. Jeff gave me a 20 gauge 311A one year for Christmas, so all I lack having a set is a .410 gauge. I've seen a couple of them at gun shows, for $500 to $700 dollars each, and maybe someday I'll decide to spend that much and get one, but for right now I just wish I had one.

There are now as many or more grey squirrels as there are Fox squirrels at Mom's farm. The grey's have even moved east and we have them at our place. For years there were two distinct species, but now the grey's and reds are cross breeding, and I see quite a few that are definitely hybrids.

* * * * *

Pappy, Sis and I used to do a lot of fishing in Nifong's pond, but it was actually more fun to fish in Little Bonne Femme Creek, we just had to walk a lot farther to get there. Pappy would tie the cane poles on the side of his '37 Chevy and we would go to the dead-end at Charlie Hall's driveway. We would then walk through the woods, along the edge of Charlie's hay field, then back up the creek to the "Mill-dam hole."

One afternoon when we were there the fish were biting so fast that one of us always had a fish on the hook. We caught bull-heads, flat-heads and big creek perch all afternoon. Sis finally got so tired she couldn't set the hook. She would just gently lift a fish out of the water, and it would jump off.

The next hole down-stream, by the old maple syrup cabin, contained a really big flat head. We'd always stop and try our luck with him, but he was pretty indifferent about our offerings. Tommy Stewart or Tom Watson finally caught the old fish. I don't remember which one.

There was a rumor that the big cat was a pasta fish; he got noodled.'

* * * * *

Back in the late 1940s and early 50's, Sis and I and Kenny and John Cavcey spent lots of time fishing in Clear Creek. Sometimes all four of us at once, sometimes just one or two, but some of us were at the creek at least 4 or 5 times a week.

Some of us had cutoff cane poles, some of us had good, peeled Hickory poles, rigged with Pappy's 30# test line and a cork. Some of the best fishing was in water that wasn't over 18" deep, so we had to use corks or we'd be on the bottom of all the time. Besides, for kids that age half the fun is watching that cork go under.

We caught lots of little bull-heads, Perch, and a few Suckers. Occasionally one of us would catch a halfway decent fish. We measured the fish on our fingers, anything as long as our finger was a keeper, and it didn't matter how small they were, if we cleaned them Mom or Grandma would fry them.

Kenny Cavcey caught the biggest Perch that I ever saw come out of Clear Creek, in the hole east of the crossing, that is now just a gravel bar. We'd been fishing with worms and getting lots of nibbles and catching an occasional baby, but nothing else. Kenny caught a grasshopper, baited up and caught that big Perch on his first toss. We didn't stay around to try for more, we were so proud of that fish that we went straight home to show it off.

One spring after a rain the creek was running pretty good, so Pappy got his cane pole and some worms and headed for the creek, with me tagging along. He started in the little hole of water under the water gap in Nifong's fence, and fished every hole of water until he got to the road. He caught more fish in two hours than the four of us kids caught the rest of the summer. It must have had something to do with experience.

* * * * *

Marcia in front of the little house, 1962.

When Marcia and I were first married we lived in a remodeled chicken house which we rented from Wat Cheavens, a couple of miles south of Pierpont. I was working construction at the time instead of farming, so I usually got home with plenty of daylight to spare, and went squirrel hunting or fishing almost every afternoon.

Wat had a lazy old Basset hound named Robbie, who always went with me if I remained close to home. When I stopped at the nearest pond he would stay as long as I did, but if I continued on he would turn around and go back to the house. One evening I headed toward the pond, catching grasshoppers as I went, with old Robbie trailing along behind. The pond had willows overhanging it about two-thirds of the way around and Bluegill could usually be caught under the willows, about three feet from the bank.

Fish were biting really slow that evening, and they were stealing three or four grasshoppers for each decent bite that I got. I caught a few small Bluegill, but finally ran out of grasshoppers. I had noticed that Robbie was carrying several fat dog ticks, as big as the end of my little finger, so I called him over and selected a nice specimen. I stuck it on the tip of the hook and made a short sideways cast under the willows. I was fishing about 18" deep, with a small bobber, and before it settled down something struck the tick hard, and headed across the pond. The way it hit I thought it was a big bass. I soon realized it wasn't, but before long I reeled in an extremely large Bluegill. It had completely swallowed the tick, hook and all.

The little house at Wat and Thelma's, 1962.

Old Robbie had wandered off, so I coaxed him back and picked off all of his ticks and dropped them in the bait can. I caught at least one, and sometimes two or three Bluegill with every tick, most of them on the first cast. They were all bigger that I usually caught out of this pond, and every one of them struck like a bass.

That was the only time I ever used dog ticks for bait, but they provided me with about thirty minutes of the hottest fishing that I have ever experienced.

Traveling Salesmen and Pass-Through Painters

I don't remember them all, but when I was a kid there was always a traveling salesman of some sort stopping at the house, some once a week, some once a month, some once and gone. Moorman's Feed, various seed salesmen, food, spices, machinery, appliances and most anything else you can think of.

The Raleigh Man(Wesselman) stopped once a month and delivered all kinds of spices; I loved to go with him when he opened the trunk of his car, it smelled like a spice factory. The Manor Man delivered bread for a while, but Mom and Grandma decided they were buying to many things they could cook themselves, so he didn't come for too much longer. It wasn't that far to Walkup's Station anyhow, if we really needed a loaf of bread.

One spring Mom bought an Electrolux vacuum cleaner from a salesman who stopped at the house. A couple of years later he went to the pen for burglary. There were others who stopped from time to time, but I don't remember who they were, or what they sold.

* * * * *

When I was a kid, a man who lived several miles southeast of us started selling feed to supplement his farm income.

Grandpap was never one to speak bad about other people, but one afternoon after he and Pappy had been subjected to an extra long spiel about the virtues of Moorman's Feed, Grandpap looked at Pappy and remarked, "William, he was a pretty good feller until he started peddling feed, now he just don't know when to hush up."

* * * * *

Once Grandpap had a pass-through barn painter from way down south paint the roof of the big barn. A retarded black boy named Willie worked for him and did the painting. That roof is pretty steep, but Willie pulled off his shoes and socks and walked around on the roof like there was nothing to it. Pappy remarked that he didn't know how Willie could stay up there. The man who owned the paint rig said "Oh, he falls off occasionally, as long as he lands on his head it don't hurt him. Don't really matter, he's got a couple of brothers just like him, if he gets hurt I can always get one of them."

Kind of a politically incorrect remark, by today's standards.

* * * * *

Some pass through barn painters are nothing but damn crooks. One year the "red barn" across the road was needing paint pretty bad. Grandpap hired a pass-through painter to spray the whole barn, roof, sides, doors and all, with aluminum roof paint. When he finished he had even sprayed the window panes aluminum. As it turned out, it didn't really matter. That barn shined like a diamond in a goat's butt until the first big rain, then it all washed off. It wasn't really paint, it was diesel fuel with a little aluminum coloring. Of course that old boy was completely out of the area by then.

Grandpap was an extremely smart man, but he was so honest in all his dealings that he expected everyone else to be honest also. Therefore, he got burnt occasionally.

Despite all that, there are some really good pass-through painters around. Jimmy Riley is the best. Jimmy isn't really a pass-through painter, he's a "come back" painter. Jimmy comes back to Boone County every spring from Tennessee, and he always has repeat customers. He's painted quite a bit for me, and even spray painted Mom's house one year. Jimmy's not afraid to come back next year, because he always does a pretty good job.

Fresh paint on my barn, thanks to Jimmy Riley.

School Boards

Serving on the school board is a really good way to piss people off. When I was first elected to the New Haven School Board it consisted of Larry McCray, Dale Pauley, Bill Blackwell, Dale Watson, and other people who had some common sense. However, it wasn't very long before the subdivision crowd started out voting the locals, and pretty soon we had bankers, college professors, Columbia businessmen and even some women on the board. That's when things pretty much went to hell.

One year some of the 8th grade girls told their parents that one of the male teachers was trying to feel them up when they were at his desk. We called a special meeting, and the parents told us what the girls had reported. The teacher then gave his side of the story. He told us that he may have "inadvertently brushed the inside of their thighs with my hand occasionally". I picked right up on that comment. I said "Mister, at one time I used to brush a thigh with my hand occasionally, but by God it was never inadvertent. That's the dumbest damn excuse I ever heard in my life!"

After we had heard all of the discussion we went into executive session, to decide what we needed to do. Old politically correct Alan said "I move we fire the son-of-a-bitch!" This motion brought gasps of horror from some of the pansy-assed board members, as they said "We can't do that, he might sue us." I replied "If that son-of-a-bitch wants to get on the witness stand and testify that we fired him for feeling up the 8th grade girls, then let that son-of-a-bitch sue."

So what did that bunch of damn wimps do? We gave the teacher a paid leave-of-absence until the end of the school year, and furnished him with a letter stating that he had been employed as a teacher at the New Haven School for xx number of years. I had very little respect for some of those board members after that, and I often wondered how many girls that son-of-a-bitch felt up before he ran into a school board with some balls.

A couple of years later some of the subdivision crowd got up a petition to annex New Haven into the Columbia School district, because our tax rate was higher than Columbia's. Some of the wimpy assed board members even came out in favor of the annexation.

It passed, we're now in the Columbia School District, and all they've done since we got there is raise taxes. I laugh every time they announce that they need another bond issue and levy increase.

*   *   *   *   *

Pappy was on the Grindstone School Board when the seven one room schools joined together to build New Haven School. It took seven attempts before the bond issue passed to build the school. The District had too many big landowners with no kids or grown kids who didn't want to pay extra tax.

By the time the school was built, all of the original board members had been voted off. They had done all of the necessary work to get the school built, but they had made a lot of people mad in the process. Like I said, serving on the school board is a really good way to piss people off.

It Must Be True: Paw-Paw Said So

New Haven School

* * * * *

When New Haven was under construction during 1955, Pappy, Hale Cavcey, and maybe one other original school board member had not yet been voted off the board by the district tight-wads.

My sister, Virginia, said that Pappy told her that the board met several times as they tried to make decisions about the teachers at the new school. New Haven was comprised of a couple of schools that had closed several years earlier, and five schools that were still open; Turner, Carter, Deer Park, Grindstone, and what was known at the time as "Colored" Grindstone. The new school needed a principal and four teachers, so with five teachers available it shouldn't have been too much of a problem, except this was 1955. What were they going to do with Eva Coleman, the teacher at "Colored" Grindstone?

President Eisenhower had recently sent National Guard troops into Little Rock, Arkansas, in an attempt to keep the peace as their schools were integrated. Columbia schools were still segregated, and this was actually going to be Boone County's first integrated school. The board definitely didn't want National Guard troops patrolling New Haven School property.

The night that the board met to offer new teacher contracts, Mrs. Coleman was the first to be interviewed. Pappy said that when she entered the room they could tell by her demeanor that she was expecting to be terminated. The board president at the time (probably Herald Barnes) informed her that she had more education than any of the other teachers, and that in a perfect world they would offer her the job of Principal. He then said "However, it isn't a perfect world, and we're afraid that Boone County isn't quite ready for a black Principal." He then told her that if she was willing to teach 3rd and 4th grades, the board was more than willing to offer her that position, and they would stand behind her 100%. Pappy said that she had tears in her eyes when she left the room.

After the first year all the parents realized that Mrs Coleman was probably the best teacher that their kids would ever have, and therefore she taught peacefully at New Haven until her retirement several years later. Over the years, she often thanked Pappy for saving her job, but it wasn't just Pappy. Hale Cavcey, Herald Barnes, Arno Winkler, and the other board members all realized that she was way too good of a teacher to lose just because of her color. Due in large part to Mrs Coleman's personality and teaching ability, this was one of the most peaceful school integrations ever accomplished.

Tractors, Machinery, and Machinery Dealers

When I was growing up, Columbia was full of farm equipment dealers. Some that I remember were:
George Russell Farm Equipment Co. - Ford
Henderson Implement Co. - Allis-Chalmers
Farmer's Implement Co. (Ferd Cottle) - John Deere
Woodward Implement Co. - Farmall IH
Vandiver Motors - Ferguson and Studebaker Cars
Wards Truck Service - Oliver
Douglas Feed Co. - Minneapolis-Moline

In later years Joe Traxler opened a Case dealership on Route N, down towards Whoop-Up. If Columbia ever had Cockshutt, Massey-Harris or B.F. Avery dealers I don't remember them.

Now there are only two full-line dealers in Columbia. Crown Power sells Case-IH and Sydenstricker Equipment sells John Deere. Both are really big dealerships. Lawn and Leisure sells LOTS of lawn equipment and they handle Kubota tractors, but they don't attempt to compete in the big tractor market. The "new" Henderson Implement Co. (no longer owned by Henry Semon) handles New Holland Equipment, but they don't sell or service combines, so I don't really consider them a full-line dealership.

From the 1940s through the 1970s every 40, 80 or 120 acre farm had a pretty complete line of machinery. Now those 40's and 80's are part of 600 to 2000 acre operations. Instead of a dozen people working ground with a 8 or 10 foot disk, one man works the same number of acres with a 35 foot disk, or maybe no-tills the ground with a 24 or 36 row planter.

The tractors that are out there are many times bigger than they used to be, but there aren't nearly as many of them so most of the dealers have been forced out of business over the years.

* * * * *

1949 was a pretty wet spring. Pappy was farming with an old 9N Ford tractor, and he was having quite a bit of trouble getting a crop planted.

It took a long time to get much ground disked with a 6 foot disk, and Pappy had worked the schoolhouse field on Nifong's twice, and each time it had rained before he could drill any beans. The next time it got dry enough to work he changed his strategy. He would disk 4 or 5 acres, unhitch from the disk, hook up to the drill and plant that strip, then switch equipment and start over. It was pretty slow, but at least he got something planted.

Pappy with his first tractor, a 9N Ford, and Mom's nephews, Kenneth and Herbert Jongebloed from New York City., 1940.

At that time we had an old 10-hole horse drill, with a stub tongue in it so it could be pulled with the tractor. I was only seven years old at the time, not really big enough to be much help, so Grandpap had to ride the drill and work all the levers. We were at the end of the field by what is now Bearfield Road, refilling the drill when George Russell came down the road with a brand new, bright shiny 8N Ford on his truck. He stopped, stuck his head out the window, and asked how to get into the field. Pappy told him, he waved, and drove on down the road.

Pappy and Grandpap were discussing who on our road might have bought a new tractor when George came pulling into the field. He unloaded, then told Pappy that he would use the old tractor and disk ground, so that Pappy could try out the new 8N while he drilled.

George disked for two days, until the field was finished, and as he left on the second day he told Pappy he would be back the next day to pick up a tractor, and said Pappy could tell him then which one to take. Naturally, Pappy told him to take the old one, and we kept that beautiful new 8N. I almost wore my butt out on that little tractor before Pappy bought an 860 Ford in the spring of 1958.

George had sold a lot of 9N and 2N tractors during the 8 years they were built, and he spent that entire spring and summer hauling new 8Ns to people who had the old ones, then working for them a couple of days while they tried out the new tractor. It was a pretty good sales ploy, because George sold a new tractor to almost everyone who tried one out.

Dealers today will bring you a demonstrator, but I can't imagine any of them spending most of the summer working for their customers.

* * * * *

The first combine Pappy had was a 4-and-a-half foot cut Case. Then he got a 5-foot cut Case, and finally a 6-foot cut Ford. He had three wagons that held 40 to 50 bushel each, plus another 20 bushel in the combine bin. That 140 to 150 bushel was usually a pretty good days cutting.

Early the next morning Ed Crawford, and later his son Harold, would bring a truck to the field and help scoop out the wagons and haul that 150 bushel to town for 5cents per bushel. Ed showed up one morning with a 3" auger with a little gas motor on it. It was pretty slow, but it sure beat scooping.

Ed would also haul hogs and calves to town for $5.00 per load. The loading chute started in the lane to the barn and ran out to the road bank. Ed would park crossways of the road, completely blocking it, while we loaded. Now I can't hardly walk cattle across the road for all the damn traffic.

* * * * *

Pappy bought his first tractor in 1939, and a combine shortly afterwards. When I had the opportunity it never occurred to me to ask how they threshed before that. They had a binder, so that got the grain cut, and my sister, Virginia, discovered that at one time Grandpap owned a quarter interest in a threshing machine, but we have no idea who his partners were. Also, I have no idea if it was powered by a steam engine or an early gas tractor, and who might have owned that. My cousin, Frank Easley, told me that he could remember a steam engine coming down the road, but he had no idea who might have owned it.

Also, when I was a kid there was an old feed grinder in the middle of the barn lot. It hadn't been used for years, and it was locked up, but the belt pulley was still on it. There was also the remains of a cream separator with a belt pulley. I assume these were run with a hit and miss engine, but I have no idea what kind it was, or what happened to it, and I didn't care enough that at the time to ask.

It's also possible that they jacked up a wheel on the car and ran everything that way, like we did the sausage grinder in later years. However, at the time I was more interested in hunting, fishing, playing baseball and chasing girls, and I didn't really care what had happened in the "old days."

Pappy also told me there was a sawmill on the farm for a while, but I didn't ask who operated it, if Pappy or Grandpap ever worked at the mill, if it was steam powered or tractor powered, or how long it was there. Damn, there are a lot of questions I would like to ask Pappy and Grandpap, if it was just possible.

*   *   *   *   *

When I was a little kid my favorite toy was a cast-iron pickup truck that Mom had bought for me at a farm auction. The last 65 years have been kind of hard on it, it's in pretty rough condition, but I still have it setting on a shelf with my other toys.

I don't remember how it happened, but somehow the back axle of the truck got broken, and I thought it was the end of the world. The next time that Pappy took plow shares to Ferd Cottle's to get them sharpened, he took my broken truck along. Tommy Sargent braised the axle and made my truck as good as new. I tried a give Tommy a penny, but he said we'd settle up after I got grown.

After Ferd Cottle sold out to Bill Johnson, Tommy worked for Columbia Welding for several years. He was welding on my combine one day, and I asked him if he remembered fixing my truck, but he didn't. Apparently it hadn't made as big of an impression on Tommy as it did on me, because I sure never forgot what he had done for me.

Some of Pappy's Machinery, mid 1950's. The Case planter on the left was converted from a horse-drawn planter to 3-point hitch by Tommy Sargent. The 2-bottom Ferguson plow in the center was bought new in 1939, along with a 9N Ford tractor. The Peorie-Union grain drill on the right had the horse tongue cut off short, for use behind the tractor. Someone still had to ride on the drill and operate the control levers.

* * * * *

The same year that Pappy bought his 860 Ford tractor, Raymond Myers bought a 560 Farmall. His 560 had some serious rear-end problems, and torque problems numerous times during the year.

It Must Be True: Paw-Paw Said So

The next spring Raymond was at the farm for some reason, and he looked at Pappy's 860 and said, "By God, Bill, I spent more money on my 560 for repairs last year than you gave for that little old Ford." Pappy looked at him and said "Raymond, it sounds to me like you might have bought the wrong kind of tractor." For once, Raymond didn't have an answer.

Stephen and Paw-Paw with Bill Blackwell's 860 Ford tractor. Pappy bought this tractor new in 1958. Bill has owned it since 1982.

* * * * *

At the first farm auction, that was held during the mid 1970s, Pappy and Mom tried to get rid of everything that hadn't been used in years, and probably wouldn't ever be used again. Chicken feeders, incubators, lard kettles, sausage grinder, lard press and hand carved lard stirring paddle, cider mill, and untold other treasures.

James Earl Grant bought the big lard kettle that was in the cellar house, and he still uses it today.

At the time, old worn out machinery was just that, old worn out machinery, and there was no collector market so most of it went to scrap buyers. A Case corn planter, Case mower, Acme harrow, John Deere grain drill, Case Sulky rake, a long-tom rake converted to push with a tractor, and many other pieces of worn out, obsolete machinery that I would love to have now, just so I could park it in a row and look at it.

I go to farm auctions now, and pay $15.00 to $25.00 for old walking plows and cultivators to set in Marcia's flower beds. At the sale we threw 10 to 15 of them into a big pile, and the whole pile probably didn't bring over two or three dollars, for scrap.

* * * * *

George Sargent, at Ferd Cottle's Farmers Implement Co. could do the best job of sharpening plow shares of anyone I ever saw. I don't remember ever walking into that shop when the old coal forge wasn't fired up ready for use.

George would shove a plow share into the coals until it was red-hot, then pull it out with the tongs and beat on it with a large hammer, reheat it, use the big trip hammer to put some "suck" into the share, then more heat, more hammering, then finally he would quench it. I never saw a share that wouldn't plow when he got done with it. I always loved to watch the sparks fly when George beat on those red-hot shares.

* * * * *

A. F. Fullington, who worked for George Russell Farm Equipment Co., and later owned the dealership himself was the best 9N through 860 Ford tractor mechanic I ever saw. The best baler mechanic was a dead heat between Henry Semon of Henderson Implement Co., and Wayne Vandeloecht of Modern Farm Equipment Co. in Fulton, MO. They were a toss-up, and they were both damn good. Henry is in his mid 80's, and he's still as good as they get.

Wayne Vandeloecht, owner of Modern Farm Equipment Co. in Fulton, Mo., was always a good person to do business with. After the Ford tractor dealerships in Columbia kind of faded out I did a lot of business with Wayne over the years, and he always treated me right.

The first time we traded tractors was a cold day in November, 1969. Wayne hauled a used 5000 Ford over to the farm, and while I was looking at it and driving it around, Wayne was checking out my 960 Ford. We'd get cold and go in the house and drink some coffee, then go back out and look at the tractors some more. Finally, by the end of the day I was the owner of a 5000 Ford tractor and a Philco-Ford portable dish washer that had been dinged pretty hard in transit. Wayne was the owner of a 960 Ford tractor and two country hams. Just before Wayne left I kicked in another $50.00, and bought a Minneapolis-Moline

Henry Semon performing emergency baler repairs, September 2008.

"Z" tractor that had been setting on his lot since spring. It was kind of like going to a swap-meet.

Reese Reeder of Modern Farm Equipment Co. on left, helping Justin and Clint examine a used combine. Clint said "You better buy it, Paw-Paw."

Olivet Neighbors

We've lost lot of good neighbors since we bought our farm in 1963. In no particular order they include: Marvin Richards, Cecil Zumwalt, Hoot Gibson, William McHarg, Jack Murphy, Fred Barnes, Herald Barnes, Henry Baumgartner, E. F.(Joe) Lawman, Raymond Smith, Harold Johnson (Harold the carpenter), Larry McCray, Arno Winkler, Charles Carl, Chub Gerard, Willis Smith, Jim Black, Martin Behymer, Floyd Vemer, David Vemer, C. J. Tekotte, R. J. Estes, J. R. Jacobs, Charlie Reid, Ancel Pace, George Williams, Henry Forsee, Wayne Delis-Denier, Vencil Sapp, Leroy Sapp, Oscar Elley, Ray Hinshaw, Bryan Mitchell, Carson Teel, Otis Warren, Jim Meyers, Ed Gordon, and Charlie Andrews.

When we first moved out here the neighbors called James Earl Grant and myself "them boys." Now we're the old timers. Except for Bandy Jacobs and Babe Manns we've been here longer than most anyone else. Damn, that just doesn't seem right.

* * * * *

Marcia and I started looking for a farm as soon as we got married. At Grandpap's funeral I was talking to Arno Winkler, who I had known all my life, and I mentioned that I heard he had bought another farm. He said he had bought one, and wanted to sell part of it. One thing led to another and a couple of months later we bought 40 acres from Arno, on what is now Turner Farm Road.

At that time 21 was the legal age when a person could sign deeds, etc. I gave Arno a $500.00 check and he held the farm for three months, until I was old enough to buy it. We built our house the first year we owned the farm, and have been here ever since. We've accumulated so much junk over the years that I wouldn't move now if someone gave us a brand new house. It would be more trouble than it was worth to load everything up.

* * * * *

When the boys were little, Marcia and I square danced for several years. Other couples from the Olivet neighborhood who danced were J.R. and Edith Jacobs, Arno and Alberta Winkler, Jim and Lorena Black and Tom and Velda Davison. Others we danced with over the years were Gary and Lynn Chandler, who now live in the Olivet neighborhood, Bob and Linda Shultz, John and Martha Strawn, Joe and Wanda Mahan and Lloyd and Helen Robinson.

Lynn & Gary Chandler, 2nd couple from left. February 1973.

We danced at least once a week, sometimes twice, and occasionally three times. It was a lot of fun, but it was pretty expensive and very time consuming, so over the years we went less and less, until we finally quit completely. Square dancing is sort of like going to church, once you quit it's kind of hard to ever get started back.

It Must Be True: Paw-Paw Said So

* * * * *

When I first started farming back in the early 1960s, I was working construction during the day, and doing my farming at night and on weekends. It's hard to get much combining done at night, so I hired my harvesting done.

One year a slick-talking salesman at MFA convinced me to try a new variety of soybean seed. They were supposedly so good that they were going to revolutionize the soybean industry. Thirty per cent better yields, better stands, better disease resistance and on and on. But they forgot to mention that the son-of-bitches popped out worse than Amsoys'.

I decided to try 25 acres of them on the old Idle Farm on Richland Road. I'm glad I didn't plant more than that, because 25 acres of them was plenty. They were taller than my other beans, had more pods, and really looked good until about 15 minutes after they matured, then they started popping out of the pods.

Raymond Myers was going to cut my beans that year, and he had indicated that he would be able to start as soon as the beans were ready, but he got started cutting Milo for Kenneth Dudley first. The elevators were covered up with Milo that fall and Raymond would cut for a day, and then set for a day or two until he could get his trucks unloaded. I told Raymond that the beans were going to hell, but he didn't want to switch his combine over to beans, and then have to switch it back to Milo. He said he would be there in about a week.

One evening after supper Cecil Zumwalt called me and asked if I had looked at my beans lately. I told him that I looked at them every day on my way home from work, and didn't really like what I was seeing. Cecil said "Alan, you need to get those things cut, you're going to loose them all." I explained the situation and told him all I could do was wait, unless he could cut them for me. He replied that he had so many beans of his own to cut that he really didn't have time.

We talked about other things for a few minutes, and just before we hung up Cecil asked me "Where do you want to take those beans, if I did get a chance to cut them?" I told him MFA, and we hung up the phones. The next day after work I went by the field to check on the condition of the beans and they were already cut. The only thing still in the field was Cecil's combine.

I called him that evening to thank him, and he said he was going past them with his combine and just didn't have the heart not to stop and cut them. That was back when most people were charging $4.50 or $5.00 per acre for combining. I asked Cecil what I owed him and he said "Oh, I was right there anyhow, $3.00 will be plenty." He didn't want to take it, but I went ahead and paid him $5.00 per acre anyhow.

Cecil was like that right up 'til the time of his death. If he owned a piece of machinery that you needed you were always welcome to use it, and he never wanted to charge you anything for it, and if you needed help Cecil was always there, even if he had things of his own that he needed to be working on. He was a hell of a good neighbor!

*   *   *   *   *

When we first moved east of town Otis and Pinky Warren lived in Charles Henry Reid's little tenant house, across Fulton Gravel Road from J.R. Jacobs. Otis worked for J. R., and usually got off at noon on Saturday.

One Saturday Charles Henry got Otis to help him during the afternoon. Charles Henry could make wine out of almost anything, and he always had a good supply on hand. When they finished working, he paid Otis with several bottles of homemade wine.

J. R. said Monday morning Otis didn't show up for work. Tuesday morning Otis didn't show up for work. J. R. said Wednesday morning around 7:00, he saw Otis walk out of his house and start across the road. It took him about 15 minutes to get to J. R.'s and when he got there he was still so sick that he wasn't much help 'till noon.

J. R. told Charles Henry "Don't ever pay Otis with wine again, or I never will get a damn crop planted."

* * * * *

We just missed an almost 100% chance of rain, and I got to thinking about Floyd Vemer. It could be too muddy to do anything for a month, but the 3rd day in a row that it was dry enough to get in the field Floyd would say "I just hope it doesn't quit raining completely." Likewise, it didn't matter how dry it had been, if it rained 3 days in a row Floyd would say "I sure hope it doesn't keep this up forever, there won't be any way we can get our crops out of the field this fall."

I was at J. R. Jacobs' place one afternoon. It had just stopped raining and we were setting in his shop watching the water run down his driveway when he remarked, "We probably didn't get much over an inch, I 'spect old Floyd is starting to worry about a drought." The old timers that lived in the neighborhood when we moved in sure made life more interesting.

One spring a few years after we moved to our place I bought some clover seed from J. R. Jacobs. I asked him if I should make the check out to him or his wife, Edith. He said "Make it to her, she's going to spend it anyway," so that's what I did. I didn't think anymore about it until that summer when J. R. cut and hauled my wheat. I went by MFA to get my check, but I hadn't sold any wheat. I had to pick up Marcia's check and bring it home to her. It's funny how things have a way of evening up.

* * * * *

One spring Turner Vemer was planting beans on his farm east of Range Line Road. During the course of the day Raymond Smith made numerous trips up and down the road for various reasons. Raymond was drinking Michelob Lite in pony bottles, and every time he passed the field he sat a cold pony on top of a fence post where Turner would be sure to see it on his next round.

Turner was lucky that Bob Bourn had a good spray truck, because by the time he finished planting that field the rows had gotten way too crooked to cultivate.

* * * * *

One of the first tractor pulls in Boone County took place at Kenneth Roberts' Station at the corner of Highway 40 and Dozier's Station Road. I-70 wasn't built yet, and Carter School Road intersected Highway 40, making it possible for people from the South to cross the highway to get to the station.

David Vemer had a nearly new Farmall 560, and he had pulled out of the hay field to fuel up at the station. While he was inside, C. J. Tekotte pulled in on his John Deere 3020. Jay walked in the store and said "Whoever owns that red piece of crap needs to move it, so I can get to the pump." David replied "If you want that son-of-a-bitch moved, hook on it and drag it out of your way." Jay replied "By God, I can do it." As they were hooking up the chain Kenneth Roberts came running out hollering at David and Jay to get the hell off his parking lot before they started acting like fools, but he was about 30 seconds to late. David and Jay drug each other back and forth the length of the parking lot for at least five minutes, digging holes in the gravel and just generally making a big old mess.

They didn't prove who had the best tractor, but they had a lot of fun, and when they were done Tekotte fueled up, and they both told Kenneth if they had time they sure would like to stay and help him smooth up his parking lot, but since they were both busy in the hay field he would just have to do it by himself.

*   *   *   *   *

Tekottee left his John Deere "50" parked in his driveway one afternoon when he went to town. While he was gone, someone (Bill Gentzsch swears it wasn't him) wired the hand clutch on the tractor so it wouldn't disengage.

The next time Jay got on the tractor he pulled on the clutch, and thinking it was disengaged he hit the starter. The tractor started immediately and headed towards an elm tree by the driveway, with Jay jerking frantically on the clutch lever. By the time he realized that the clutch wasn't going to work, the tractor was trying to climb that elm tree. Jay had the presence of mind to turn off the ignition switch, bringing everything to a halt.

That was a hell of a good prank, and I wish I had thought of it myself, but old Tekotte was really lucky the tractor didn't climb that tree far enough that it flipped over backwards on him.

* * * * *

Greg and Jeff learned a lot of good words from Tekotte when they were growing up. They called him "old cusser."

One day the boys and I were visiting with Jay out by his barn, when John Deere salesman Junior Riley drove in. He had been trying to sell Jay a loader for his John Deere 50, and he had come back to try to finalize the deal.

Tekotte and Junior sat down on the tailgate of Jays pickup and started talking business. They weren't but $25.00 apart on price, but you'd have thought it was $10,000.00. For the next half hour they questioned each others' ancestry, sexual preferences, occupation (crook, thief, conman, shyster), sometimes all of the above in the same sentence.

The louder they got, the quieter the boys got. Finally, Jeff asked "Daddy, are they going to fight?" I said "Don't worry, neither one of them have enough sense to know how to make a fist." They finally compromised on price and Jay bought the loader. He had it for years, and it finally sold at his sale, after he passed away.

* * * * *

Jay and Ruth Tekotte and Harold and Beulah Johnson were neighbors for many years, and Jay and Beulah were usually crossways with each other about something. One spring they had been at it again, so when Jay started cleaning out his sheep barn he waited until there was a good stiff breeze out of the South, then he spread several loads of that nasty smelling, soured sheep manure across the road from Johnson's house.

A couple of days later Harold saw Jay and told him "I wish you and my wife would iron out your differences, because that sheep crap smells so bad I can't hardly stand it."

The smell went away in a few days, but that wasn't the only time it happened. Over the years that field across the road from Harold's house had more sheep manure spread on it than all of the other fields on Jay's farm put together. Beulah never did learn that when someone has a barn full of sheep crap and a manure spreader, it's best if you don't get them pissed off.

* * * * *

One spring Doc Kinkead had some really common looking Holstein steers on the 55 acres that Charlie Reid still owned, north of Ed Gordon's.

There wasn't any decent fence on the place, and Doc had strung a hot wire to keep his calves in. He asked Tekotte if he could drive the calves across the road into Jay's pens, to load them out. Jay said he could, if he would do it at night. He told Doc "I don't want someone to see those sorry son-of-a-bitches over here, and think that they're mine." Doc said "Tekotte, you've owned cattle that were just as common as these." Jay replied "Yeah, but the son-of-a-bitches all died, and I didn't have to load them out."

It's a good thing Doc Kinkead is a veterinary, because when he had the place on Olivet Road that Marilyn Brown owns now he used to stock it with some pretty raggedy-assed looking calves. There's no way someone could afford to hire a vet to keep calves like those alive.

He would buy calves from Texas or Oklahoma, where ever they were cheapest and dump them all together, his theory being "Expose 'em to everything, the ones that live will have a hell of a good immune system."

I guess he was right, because over the years he bought and sold more cattle than most of us ever see.

When Doc closed his clinic north of I-70 it sure made working cattle in this area a whole lot more inconvenient.

* * * * *

Tekotte had a lot of trouble with dogs killing his sheep. He said if you raised sheep you needed two things, a shotgun and a post hole digger. You could always tell when dogs had been in his sheep, there would be a couple of new corner posts around his pens somewhere. Jay said a dog in the bottom of a post hole couldn't cause hard feelings between neighbors.

* * * * *

Years ago, when our boys were still small, Marcia and I, along with three other couples, decided to take our kids for a hay ride on Halloween, rather than sending them out to go trick or treating. I don't remember how many kids there were, but counting our two I assume there were eight or ten involved.

It was pretty cold that night, but after snuggling down amongst the hay bales and loose straw everyone seemed fairly comfortable, except for the poor old tractor driver. We had made it down the road almost to the farm of Jay and Ruth Tekottte, and since Jay and I played pranks on one another on a fairly regular basis, I decided this was too good of a chance to pass up.

When I reached their driveway I slowed down and turned in, cut across the frozen yard, and stopped as close to the back door as I could get. I got off the tractor and knocked, and when Jay opened the door I said "Old man, I've got some trick or treaters' on the wagon have you got anything for them?" He asked how many there were and I replied that I hadn't counted, but there must be at least thirty or forty of them. Jay looked at me and said "Good Lord, Bud, we've got a little candy, but not enough for thirty or forty kids."

I could see past him into the kitchen, where several people I didn't know were seated around the table, and just past them on the kitchen counter, with steam still rising form them were three pumpkin pies. I brushed past Jay and stepped over to the counter, picked up two pies and said "Don't worry about it, Old Man, I'd rather have pumpkin pie than candy, any day." As I went out the door I could hear Ruth yelling "Alan Easley, you get back in here with my pies, right now!"

I handed the pies to someone on the wagon, then jumped on the tractor and headed out the driveway. We completed the road portion of the hay ride, then drove to our pond where we fired up a brush pile so the kids could roast hot dogs and marshmallows. When they finally got filled up we returned to the house, made some coffee, then the kids played while the adults sat around the kitchen table drinking coffee and eating pie.

Over the next couple of hours we all took turns calling Ruth, to congratulate her on the quality of her pumpkin pies.

* * * * *

On the Halloween following the great pumpkin pie theft, Marcia and I once again took our boys around the neighborhood trick or treating. After visiting several homes we arrived at the Tekotte farm for the final stop on our tour.

When the boys got out of the car, instead of taking their regular trick or treat bags, I sent them to the door holding an empty MFA feed sack between them. When Ruth came to the door she recognized them immediately, and gave them an extra heavy ration of treats. As they turned to leave she asked them to please wait a minute, then she went into the kitchen and got a stale biscuit and dropped it into the sack. She said, "Tell your Daddy I don't have any pumpkin pie, he'll have to get by with an old cold biscuit."

Old Jay must have told everyone he saw what Ruth had done, because over the next several days at least a dozen people asked me about my Halloween biscuit. It was such a nice biscuit that I didn't want to throw it away, so I wrapped it up and stored it in the refrigerator for a couple of weeks. Since I couldn't figure out a good use for it, I decided to return it to its original owner. I found a small box, inserted the biscuit, gift wrapped it, stamped it, then addressed it to Ruth and put it in the mailbox.

Jay told me later, "Bud, you got a good one on her that time." He was headed toward the house from his sheep barn when he noticed Ruth coming back from the mailbox. He said "Bud, that old woman was coming down the driveway real slow, turning something over and over in her hand and looking at it, then holding it up to her ear and shaking it, then looking at it some more." He asked her what she had, and she replied "A real pretty little package, but I don't know what it is, or who sent it." They went into the house, and Ruth went to the kitchen counter and opened her package. Jay said she just stood there looking at it, and he finally asked her what it was. She replied, "Oh, that no good Alan Easley sent my biscuit back."

Jay and Ruth have been gone for many years now, but for as long as she lived Ruth was always trying to figure out a way to get even with me for some prank or the other that I had pulled on her. She usually came out ahead in the long run.

* * * * *

The first year we lived out here Arno Winkler was having back problems, and Tekotte rented part of Arno's place across from our house.

One day Marcia was mowing the yard in her bathing suit when Jay came over to disk. It wasn't to long before he walked across the road carrying his water jug and told Marcia he had spilled his drinking water, and asked her if she would refill his jug.

Jay told Arno later "that young feller's wife was mowing her yard in a bikini, so I dumped out my drinking water and got her to fix me some more." Knowing Tekotte, there's no doubt in my mind that's exactly what he did.

* * * * *

I was helping Jay combine soybeans one afternoon when the temperature was around 10 degrees, with a nice stiff breeze out of the North. My 303 International didn't have a cab heater, but with the sun shining through all the windows it was fairly comfortable.

Jay's 45 John Deere didn't have a cab, and he had on so many clothes he could hardly move, and he was still freezing. Once when he pulled up to the truck to unload I stopped back a ways, stripped to the waist and hung my tee shirt where it was easy to get to. I pulled up where Jay could see me, then made a big issue out of grabbing the tee shirt and wiping sweat off of my face. I could see Tekotte's lips moving, but what with two combines running and my cab door shut I couldn't hear a word he was saying, but knowing him I'm sure it was pretty colorful.

* * * * *

When Greg and Jeff were little no one had started using chemicals on soybeans, so the boys could play in the dirt in the field across from our house. They would take their toy tractors and implements across the road nearly every day, that was a lot more fun than playing in their sandbox.

Tekotte told his wife "Old woman, when you drive past that young feller's house you watch real close, 'cause there's a couple of little brown bunnies that run back and forth across the road all the time."

* * * * *

When Marcia and I moved to our farm east of town in 1963, Dirty Elmer and his wife lived in a two room shack just down the road from us. They had 30 some cats, and the cats all stayed in the house with them. There were no screens on the windows, so they kept the house shut up year around, so the cats couldn't get away.

Once a day Elmer walked an eighth of a mile to an old abandoned cistern well, raked off the scum and the bugs and dipped up two buckets of water. That was their drinking water, cooking water and washing water for the day. It definitely wasn't enough to take care of the washing part.

One fall evening Elmer walked over to the house and told me his heating stove wasn't working. Boone County Oil Co. had told him to bring in the name, model and serial number of the stove and they would order parts for him. Elmer and his wife couldn't read or write, and he wanted me to come over and write down the information for him. I told him I would be over shortly, so he wandered back home.

When I got there I stepped up onto the porch and I could see Elmer, his wife and about a dozen cats eating supper. The cats were on the table eating out of the serving bowls. As I watched, Elmer slapped a cat out of his way, so he could get another helping of whatever was in the bowl.

I knocked, and when Elmer opened the door I started in. The stench hit me like a sledge hammer and I stepped back, took the biggest breath I ever took in my life, ran to the stove and wrote down all of the necessary information, ran back out and then finally breathed again. That's the last time I ever want to step foot in a place like that.

* * * * *

Elmer had several DWI's over the years, and the state had permanently relieved him of his Driver's License. The first fall that we lived on the farm Elmer came to me, explained that he worked 4 hours per day at the Columbia Cemetery, and asked if he could ride to town with me. I told him he could ride to the closest point that was handy for me, and he would need to walk from there. That beat walking the whole six miles to town, so he agreed.

Elmer took a bath, shaved and changed clothes every two weeks, whether he needed to or not. Judging by the smell he definitely needed to, but we made it pretty good during the late summer and fall, because the truck windows were down, and the breeze pretty much carried the smell out the window. However, the first really cool morning was a different story. The windows were up, the heater was on and pretty soon the smell was unbearable. I turned the heater off, opened my window, and turned the vent window so that it blew on Elmer. He never said a word.

When we got to the corner where I usually let him out I stopped, and when he got out, but before he could shut the door, I said, "Elmer, we've got to make some changes. You're going to have to clean up more often, you stink so bad I can't stay in the truck with you." He looked at me and said "Well I'll be God damned," and slammed the truck door so hard it's a wonder the window didn't fall out, then turned and stomped off down the street.

Elmer and his wife lived in the shack for another year and a half before they moved and he never spoke to me again. If I'd have known it was that easy to get rid of him I'd have told him that he stunk a long time before I actually did.

* * * * *

When Marlon Landhuis bought the place Greg Michalson has now, and decided to farm it himself, it was a disaster waiting to happen. He didn't know anything about farming or machinery, and he kept practicing what he didn't know until he got worse at it.

He called me one day and said he had gotten stuck while mowing a pond bank, and needed a pull. I liked to keep as much distance between myself and Marlon as possible, but I went over to pull him out. He had been bush-hogging the pond dam on the water side, and had sunk one side of his tractor. Water was completely over the axle on the lower side, if he'd had enough sense to realize that it could turn over it would have, but God protects kids and idiots.

I pulled him out, then told him that what he was doing was dumb as hell, and a really good way to get hurt or killed. I told him if he had to mow on the water side of the dam to use a sickle mower, so he could keep the tractor on top of the bank. He agreed that would be a better way to do it, and I headed for home while he stood there looking at his mud covered tractor. A couple of days later I saw J. R. Jacobs, and he said he had seen me leaving "Dummy's Place" on my tractor a couple of days before. He said about 20 minutes after I left Marlon came over, said he was stuck, and needed a pull.

J. R. said when he got to the pond, Marlon had made it about 10 feet past the first set of ruts before sliding into the water again. J. R. asked Marlon if I had just pulled him out, and he said I had. J. R. told him he would pull him out this time, and then said "If you ever call me over here again and you're in that pond, I'm going to shove the damn tractor on in far enough that it will turn over and sink, hopefully with your dumb ass on it."

That's the kind of relationship Marlon had with most of his neighbors. Someday when you have plenty of time to listen, ask James Earl Grant about Marlon.

* * * * *

One year Marlon had 50 or 60 acres of wheat on his farm, and somehow managed to get it harvested all by himself. After he finished combining he decided he should have someone bale a few bales of straw, so he would have some if he needed it.

I don't have any idea where he got a rake, but he borrowed one from some poor soul, and raked several windrows across one end of the field without destroying the rake. Just as he finished raking, James Earl Grant came down the road with his tractor and baler.

Marlon flagged him down and asked how much he would charge to bale some straw. James Earl told him that he didn't have time to fool with it. Marlon said "You're already here, how much will you charge?" James Earl told him that he had hay raked and waiting for him, and he didn't have time to fool around baling straw. By now Marlon was getting a little indignant. He said "I told you I need it baled, how much will you charge?" James Earl said "By God, 75 cents per bale." This was back when most people were charging 25 cents per bale, if the hay was already raked. Marlon said "OK", and James Earl realized he had committed himself, so he pulled in and baled around 100 bales of straw, collected his money, and went on down the road.

A few days later Marlon told J. R. Jacobs that as expensive as baling was, he didn't know how J. R. could afford to have so much hay baled every year. When Marlon told J. R. that he had paid 75 cents per bale to get his straw baled J. R. looked at him, and as serious as possible he said "You should have got Easley, he just charges 10 cents per bale." Marlon exploded, and for the next two or three weeks he told everyone who would listen what a big crook James Earl was, and how bad he had screwed him. James Earl finally cornered Marlon at the sale barn and explained the facts of life to him. Marlon kind of calmed down after that, but he never did get over it.

As for J. R., whenever someone mentioned the feud he just laughed to himself. No one ever accused J. R. of not being an agitator.

* * * * *

One fall J. R. was sowing wheat for Marlon. The forecast was for rain, and J. R. knew he didn't have enough seed to finish. Marlon offered to take J. R.'s truck and go after more seed wheat, so that J. R. could keep drilling and maybe get done before it rained. J. R. could think of a dozen reasons why he didn't want Marlon driving his pickup, but for some reason he said o.k.; Marlon left with the truck, returned pretty much on time with enough seed to finish, and J. R. got done drilling before the rain started. Everything seemed to have worked out perfectly until the next morning.

J. R. was sitting at the kitchen table drinking coffee and listening to the rain when his phone rang. He answered, and a woman asked if he was J. R. Jacobs. When he said yes she started cussing him out. He said later that she must have been in the Navy, because she sure knew all the right words

When she finally stopped to get her breath, J. R. said "Lady, what in the hell is your problem?" " If I've got a cussing coming, o.k., but I don't even know why you're mad." She said it was about her "damn mailbox." When J. R. asked what mailbox she replied "The one you ran over with your goddamn truck, you know what mailbox."

This was back when the State required all pickup trucks to have the owners name and address on the side. Marlon had run off the road and knocked her mail box down while she was standing just a few feet away. He stopped, apologized, told her he was J. R. Jacobs and said he was in a really big hurry, but that he would call her that night and make arrangements to fix the mailbox.

J. R. fixed the mailbox at his own expense, with no help from Marlon, who just kind of acted like the whole thing had never happened.

* * * * *

J. R. always had a big sweet corn patch. He would pick half a truck load of corn 2 or 3 times a week, and go around town selling to the grocery stores.

One day he was heading towards the road on his tractor when Marlon pulled in and asked if he could get a mess of sweet corn. J. R. said he didn't have time to fool with it, but that the West side of the patch was ready if Marlon wanted to pick some himself.

Later that day I was changing the oil on one of my tractors when Marlon pulled in and asked if we needed some roasting ears. I told him the coons had stripped my patch, and that I would love to have some. He said "I've got so much I don't know what to do with it, take all you want."

I walked over to his truck, and there must have been 400 ears of corn in the bed. I took two or three dozen, thanked him, and he headed down the road to the next house. He gave away half a load of corn that afternoon, and never mentioned the fact that he had gotten it from J. R.'s patch.

The next morning J. R. was going to pick corn to sell. He said "That son-of-a-bitch had picked every ear that was ready to pick. I had to call the stores and tell them that I didn't have any corn for them."

A few years later Marlon got shot in the back when someone attempted to rob an illegal poker game that he was participating in. J. R. wasn't very sympathetic. He told Marlon "You son-of-a-bitch, you're lucky I didn't shoot you, I'd have shot you between your damn eyes!"

After Marlon got shot a bunch of neighbors got together and harvested his crop. Front Row: WIllis Smith, Russell Level, J.R. Jacobs and Alan Easley. Back Row: Turner Vemer, Jim Black, Bandy Jacobs, Martin Behymer, Babe Manns, Cecil Zumwalt, and Luke Youngman. October 5, 1980. Columbia Missourian photo by Murry Koodish, used with permission of the Columbia Missourian.

* * * * *

With neighbors like ours, we never know what kind of Holiday decorations we might have. A few years ago the head and neck of a goose decoy appeared next to the barn-lot gate, neatly wired to the fence. A couple of weeks later the goose was suddenly wearing a little red Santa hat with a white tassel. A few days after Christmas the old goose flew back to where ever he came from. We never did know for sure who was responsible, but I have my suspicions.

One year Jeff Bradley dug a hole in his front yard and built a little decorative pond, complete with a pump and water fall. One day when he wasn't home someone set out a bank line in the pond, with a shiny little red and white plastic bobber. I don't know if they caught anything, but it sure looked good from the road.

*   *   *   *   *

When Hartley and Nancy Banks lived in their "little log cabin" in Callaway County they were way to far east to be considered "Olivet Neighbors," but this story HAS to go somewhere, so here it is.

Hartley called me one spring and said he was tired of bush-hogging grass. He said if I would go to the sale barn and buy some calves he would pay for them, I could haul them and look after them, and we'd split the profit half and half. I had more time than money, and most of the money I had was borrowed from Hartley's bank, so it seemed like a pretty good idea to me.

His fence was like 90% of the fence in the world, pretty much junk, but I drove a few posts and patched it up enough to make it look functional. I brought 12 or 15 head of black white-faced steers and turned them out in Hartley's pasture. They didn't cause any problems until the day someone forgot about the calves, and left the gate open when they went fishing. Hartley called me and said the calves were scattered "all over the god damn county."

By the time I got there they had gotten the calves off the blacktop, and most of them were back in the pasture. We got three more in, then counted and discovered we were still one short. We were wandering around looking for the calf when we suddenly spotted him running across Hartley's yard with a neighbor's dog chasing him. The garage door was open and the calf ran inside, where Nancy's restored 1955 Ford Thunderbird convertible was parked, with the top down. I hollered at

Hartley to run him out before he tore the car up. Hartley said "F___ that car" and hit the button on the garage door closer. Hartley said "We've got that son-of-a-bitch caught, go get your trailer."

It took me at least a half hour to get the trailer, and when I got back I could hear the calf banging around in the garage. I opened the back gate on the trailer and backed up to the garage door. Hartley opened the door and I slipped into the garage and picked my way through rakes, shovels, garbage cans, flower pots and lawn chairs that the old steer had scattered around on the floor, and ran him into the trailer.

The Thunderbird had a couple of dents in it, but nothing real serious. However, a Ford Thunderbird is low enough that a 550# steer can crap right over the top of the doors, and the inside of that beautiful little car was well splattered with juicy, green calf crap.

I asked Hartley if he wanted me to take the calf to the sale barn while it was loaded, but he said, "Hell no, it's not his fault some dumb bastard left the gate open. Put the sorry son-of-a-bitch back in the pasture." The calves stayed there with no problem for the rest of the summer, but Hartley's first venture into the cattle business wasn't very lucrative. The calves gained quite a bit of weight but it was one of those years when the price went down all summer, so when we sold them he wound up with about $60.00 profit, which was half mine. It probably cost a lot more than $30.00 to get all of the calf crap cleaned out of Nancy's Thunderbird.

* * * * *

In the mid-1970's, Eutsy Johnson called, and wanted me to plow 75 acres on his place and sow it in wheat for him. The field was located across the creek to the north from where Old Hawthorne Golf Course is located now.

The day I went to look at the ground I noticed rocks in the bottom of a little drainage ditch where we entered the field. I asked, "Mr. Johnson, are there any rocks on this ground?" He replied "No, no, rocks have never been a problem here."

I didn't have a spring-trip plow at that time, my plow had 5/16-inch shear bolts, and I broke 47 of them before I got that damn 75 acres plowed. If rocks weren't a problem on that ground, I'd sure hate to plow ground where they were a problem.

* * * * *

A couple of years after that, I had hay mowed down in the southwest field on the Murphy Farm, across the fence from Eutsy's.

One morning when I pulled into the field to see if the hay was dry enough to rake I noticed Eutsy walking around amongst his cattle. As soon as I got out of my truck he called out "Easley, have you got cattle over there?" I replied "Not yet, but I'm going to turn some in as soon as I get this hay baled." Eutsy said "Cows are alright, but don't put a bull over there, I've got registered cattle on my place." Before I could reply he turned his back and walked away.

That was the wrong thing to do! I didn't even wait 'till I got the hay baled. As I pulled out of the field I wired the gate open and called my cattle. Eutsy and Nancy left on vacation the next morning and were gone for 30 days. James Earl Grant and I went after my bull three times that month.

Eutsy had registered Murry Grey cows, and I had a roan Shorthorn bull. The next year after he worked Eutsy's cattle, Doc Kinkead told me "I believe your bull enjoyed himself when he was at Eutsy's. There were six nice grey roan calves over there that sure didn't match the rest of the calf crop."

* * * * *

When I was 6 or 7 years old, Pappy hired Forrest Warren to build a large closet on the outside of the house. Forrest said that he'd built a lot of inside closets, but he'd never built one on the outside of a house before. At that time George Williams was working for Forrest, and I spent most of my days pestering him. Why this? Why that? Why not? George just kept smiling and answered all my questions, no matter how dumb they were. I thought he was about the neatest grown-up I had ever met.

Mr. And Mrs. George Williams, 1998

When I got a little older I went to school with some of George's kids, and Greg and Jeff went to school with some of his Grandkids. After Marcia and I got married and moved east of town we lived just a few miles from him. George ran a trash route and he picked up our trash for many years. One summer Randy Blackwell was helping me put up hay, and we mowed and baled several acres for George, on his farm southeast of Deer Park.

For years I would sell George tickets to the Olivet Bar-B-Q every summer, and a couple of weeks later he would come by and sell me tickets to the Sugar Grove Bar-B-Q. I always told him if it wasn't for Sugar Grove,

Olivet would have the best Church Bar-B-Q in Boone County.

When George passed away I went to his visitation, and there were nearly as many white people there as there were blacks. George was respected by everyone who knew him. I really miss him, he was one of those people that you just really enjoyed being around.

* * * * *

Bill Schuler and R. J. Estes were both willing to take a sip of good whiskey if it was available. One afternoon Bill pulled in at R. J.'s with a full fifth of whiskey in his truck.

R.J. walked out of his machine shed and got in the truck with Bill, where they sat for the next hour, passing the bottle back and forth. R. J.'s wife, Alice, had been in town and Bill and R. J. were still sitting in the truck when she got home.

They saw her pull in the driveway, and R. J. decided he probably should get out and talk to her. The only problem was, when his feet hit the ground his legs wouldn't hold him up, and he kind of collapsed in a pile on the driveway. Alice saw him fall and she stomped over to the truck but she didn't say a word to R. J., she just started raising hell with Bill for getting R. J. drunk. Bill looked at her and said "Why you damned old spook, he's a big boy, I didn't twist his damn arm and make him drink it."

The name stuck. R. J. was sober by the next morning, but for the rest of her life the neighbors referred to Alice as "Spooky Alice," or "Old Spook."

* * * * *

Zane Dodge and VAC Case

When the boys started school at New Haven Donna Dodge was the kindergarten teacher. We've known Zane and Donna, and now Zane and Marilyn, ever since. I sort of feel bad for not mentioning Zane more in this book, but he's almost too polite and well-mannered to write about. It's a lot easier to write about someone who is a little bit rowdy, a little bit off the wall, or just a plain old pain in the ass. Zane is none of the above, so about all I can say about him is that he's been a hell of a good friend and neighbor for the past 40 years. He's a right decent shade tree mechanic, too.

* * * * *

I was talking to Bill Blackwell on the phone late afternoon on December 31, 2011. I told him to be careful and not party too hard that night. He said it would have to be before 9:30, because that's when he usually folds up for the night.

That's quite a bit different that it used to be. Marcia and I, Bill and Doris, James Earl and Dorothy Grant, Larry and Dolores McCray, Gary and Lynn Chandler, Fuzz and Sandy Nichols, Don and Linda Duffy, Charles and LuAnna Andrews and others spent many New Years Eves at Good Time country, and lots of Saturday nights at the Optimist Club. We would close the place down around 2:00AM, then go to a restaurant or some ones house for breakfast, and get home in time to get in bed around 6:00 am.

I still get in bed around 6:00 AM lots of mornings, but it's because I had to get up at 5 minutes 'till 6:00 and pee. An extra forty years sure changes your perspective.

New Years Eve, 1978

Kids

Several years before Pappy passed away he had surgery one fall, and was unable to care for his cattle when winter came.

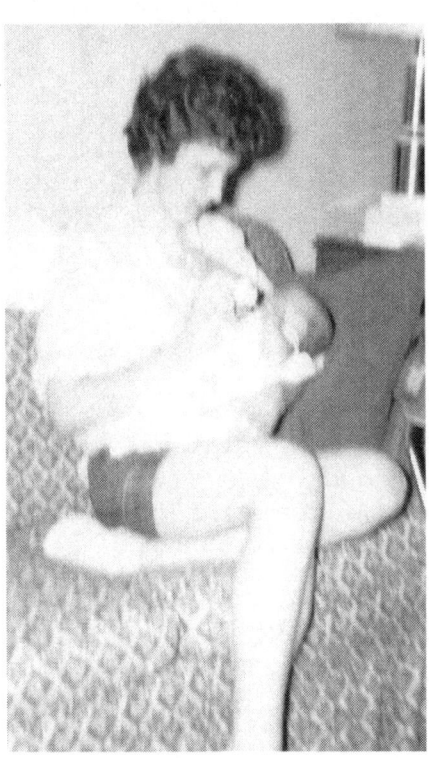

Marcia and Greg, 1963

I was still working construction at the time, and was employed in Marshall, Missouri, that winter. What with the short days and a two hour's drive after work it was a little unhandy getting the feeding done, but I worked out a pretty good system. On Sunday I would feed enough for half the week, and load up enough for the other half. Then Wednesday night, I would go by and unload in the dark. Pappy's old pets didn't get all the attention they were used to, but at least they got fed.

Pappy had a barn loft full of two year old baled oats which the mice had been working on pretty hard, so I decided I would feed them out for him before I started on the new hay.

One Sunday afternoon Greg and Jeff, who were approximately six and eight years old at the time, went with me when I fed. Occasionally a bale would have both twines intact, but most of them had only one and had to be retied, and some had no twine at all. It seemed like nearly every broken bale that I moved exposed a nest of baby mice. They ranged from little pink slugs with their eyes still closed, to somewhat older ones which were starting to grow a pretty good coat of hair. The boys thought they were in heaven.

After playing with the mice for a while they decided it would be "pretty neat" to take some to school with them on Monday, to show their friends. They went to the house and Mom found a couple of old shoe boxes which they lined with oat chaff, then each of them proceeded to collect about a dozen mice of assorted sizes.

Jeff and Greg with Lambchop and Mutton. Dirty Elmer's shack is in the background.

When we got home with the mice Marcia found an old eye dropper, warmed up some milk, and started feeding them. A baby mouse doesn't eat much at one time and it took several feedings, but except for a few of the smallest ones they survived until morning. When the school bus arrived the boys climbed aboard, proudly carrying their boxes of mice.

Not long after the bus arrived at school Marcia received an irate phone call from Gene Nichols, the principal. He was pretty upset. He asked "Marcia, do you know what your boys brought to school this morning?" She replied "Sure Gene, they had a couple of shoe boxes full of baby mice. I fed them with an eye dropper several times yesterday, so they would still be alive this morning." He said, "I don't see how you could stand to do something like that, they were the most disgusting things I ever saw. Please don't EVER send mice to school again! They almost made me sick before I could get rid of them."

Apparently as soon as the boys arrived at school they had started showing their mice to everyone they saw. The boys laughed, the girls screamed, the teachers screamed, and some of them made mad dashes to the restroom to be sick. The mice were quickly disposed of down one of the bathroom stools, and everything eventually returned to normal.

The boys were pretty disappointed about losing their mice, and they just couldn't understand what the big problem was. I really couldn't either, but I wish I had been there to see it. I think it would have been a lot of fun to watch.

* * * * *

Greg & house calf, Easter 1978. That little baby was cold, he fell in the creek.

There wasn't a whole lot of traffic on the roads when the boys were growing up. Greg and Jeff, Randy and Brent Blackwell and Kevin Brown all started riding dirt bikes on the road when they were 10 or 11 years old. Greg used hay hauling money and bought his first Mustang when he was 14. All five of those boys were driving all over the neighborhood by the time they were 13 or 14. That wouldn't work today. Now it seems like everyone who owns a car thinks they need to drive on Range Line or Turner Farm Road. If those 5 boys still had every Mustang they wrecked or mechanically destroyed while they were growing up, none of them would need to work for a living.

* * * * *

Jeff, Norm Beal and Randy Blackwell went on a mailbox bashing tour one night. Stupid was their biggest problem, but there were two others: they did it close enough to home that I knew some of the people whose boxes got bashed, and they got caught.

The next morning around 6:30 A.M. I got a call from Al Brittain, who farmed south of our place several miles, and was also a Special Deputy for the county. His son Randy was the same age as Greg. Al said he could keep things on hold until 5:00 P.M., and if I called by 5:00 and let the Sheriff's Department know that arrangements had been made to repair or replace the boxes that would be the end of it, but otherwise he would have to file charges.

Luckily the dummies got caught after messing up only three boxes. Cecil Barnes had a large box covered with an IH farm scene decal. We knocked on Cecil's door and when he answered, I introduced him to Jeff, then I went back to my truck. Jeff wasn't very happy about having to talk to Cecil, but he got it done. A couple of days later I sat in my air-conditioned pickup while Jeff and Norm replaced Cecil's mail box.

If it hadn't been for Al, those dumbasses would have been in a lot of trouble over that little episode.

It Must Be True: Paw-Paw Said So

* * * * *

When Jeff was in high school and for several years afterwards, he drove way too fast all of the time. He had a beautiful 1965 Ford Mustang convertible that would really run, and he always drove the hell out of it. One day as he was heading towards town at a high rate of speed he met a Highway Patrolman.

Jeff didn't exactly run, he just kept on driving. He figured by the time the Patrolman got turned around he would be safely out of sight. When he got to old Hwy. 63 he decided to turn north and go to the Bull Pen Cafe and lay low for a while. What Jeff didn't know was that he had met Eddie Lane, and that Eddie's wife and mother ran the Bull Pen. When Eddie didn't catch up with Jeff he decided to stop at the Cafe and visit with his wife and mother for a few minutes. Jeff had parked and gone inside and was quietly drinking a cup of coffee when a patrol car pulled into the lot and parked next to his Mustang. Eddie checked the car over real good, ran the plates and then walked into the restaurant.

The crowd consisted of farmers, construction workers, a few bankers and businessmen in fancy suits, and one high school kid in a sleeveless Harley Davidson tee shirt. Eddie looked the crowd over, and it didn't take him long to decide who he wanted to talk to. He walked up to the table and asked Jeff if he was driving the Mustang convertible. When he said he was Eddie asked to see his drivers' license. Eddie looked at it, then asked "Which Easley are you? I went to school with Alan Easley, are you any kin to him?" Jeff said he thought "Oh, boy, he knows Dad, I'm going to get out of this." When he told Eddie I was his Dad, Eddie remarked "When he was your age he drove like a damn idiot, too."

Eddie wrote Jeff a ticket for driving 85 in a 55 zone, then sat down at the table with him and ordered a cup of coffee, then visited with Jeff while they drank their coffee. Jeff said that was one time that being my son probably hurt more than it helped.

OOPS!

* * * * *

When I bought my first 4WD pickup in 1977, I sold Greg my old green and white '67 Ford pickup. Greg and his friend 'Bama hauled a lot of firewood on it for a couple of years. The night the old truck got retired, Greg went off of WW, and hit the concrete corner post between Bandy Jacob's farm and Hoot Gibson's. The Highway Patrolman told me Greg had been off the road for 100 feet before he hit the post. I went back the next day to look at things in daylight, and discovered he had been off the road on the other side for 300 feet, then jumped the road and continued on for 100 before hitting the post and flipping upside down. I knew the old truck would move right along, but he must have really had a fire built under it that night.

It was his 18th birthday, and I guess he ate something at the Easley Cave party that didn't agree with him, because he sure wasn't seeing very good that night. Before the Highway Patrol showed up Marcia took him to the hospital for stitches. As soon as we arrived at the scene, Kim Kinkead grabbed my arm and told me she had thrown away everything in the truck that might get Greg in trouble. I just thanked her, and didn't even ask what she had tossed, I didn't really want to know.

* * * * *

Jeff is on disability retirement from the City of Columbia, thanks to a sorry-assed Workmen's Comp. doctor, and a couple of back surgeries that didn't really work as planned. He lives on the old home place on Bearfield Road that has been in the family since the 1840s. Jeff has loved motorcycles since he was a little kid. On his good days he is still able to ride, and he loves to attend bike rallies.

Paw-Paw and his pets, 2010

I had fed cattle by myself for so many years that when Jeff moved into the old house it didn't even occur to me that I now had a source of help. One morning as I was letting myself through a gate with a bale of hay he walked across the road and remarked that he'd be glad to help me if he knew when I was there.

Since then I've always let him know. He rides in the back of the truck and dumps range cubes while I drive, then he works the gate and cuts net-wrap off the bales when I come through with them.

A bunch of pet yearlings, hoping that I've got some cookies in my pocket. October 2008.

One morning one of his motorcycle friends called him while he was working the gate. After Jeff told his friend what he was doing his friend said "Easy, I didn't know you were into cattle ranching." Jeff replied that when he was young and in good physical condition there were too many girls to chase, motorcycles to ride and Ford Mustangs to race, and he just didn't have time for cows.

He said now that every part of his body hurts when he climbs in and out of the truck and dumps feed sacks that he kind of enjoys doing it. I'm glad that he does, it sure makes it easier for me to feed.

Norm Beal

When Jeff was in high school one of his friends, Norm Beal, lived with us for about a year and a half. Norm's Dad and step-mom were drinking quite a bit, and Norm just couldn't get along with them, especially his step-mom. Norm showed up at the house one evening needing a place to sleep, and wound up camping in our basement until after he graduated from high school. He's almost like having another son. Norm moved to Florida and we don't see him near often enough, but it's always great when he does get here for a few days. He named his son Nicolas Alan. How about that? It made me pretty damn proud.

Norm and Jeff

Party Lines

For quite a few years after we moved to our farm east of town we were on a party line. At times we were lucky and there would only be 3 or 4 people on the line, but occasionally there would be as high as 12 families on one line. If everyone cooperated it worked o.k., even with a lot of people, but one line-hog could ruin it for everyone.

One year for some unknown reason, Raymond and Dorothy Smith wound up on our line, even though they were quite a ways southeast of us. Their oldest daughter Barbara was in high school, and she spent a lot of time on the phone talking to her boyfriend. I never knew for sure where he worked, but I assumed it was at the desk of one of the motels in Columbia, because he was always working in the evenings, but he seemed to have an unlimited amount of time to talk on the phone.

One evening when I needed to use the phone to check with my hay haulers, Barbara was having a marathon conversation with her boyfriend. The first couple of times I waited about 5 minutes between checks, but the longer they talked the oftener I checked the line. I was getting pretty aggravated and apparently Barbara was too.

The last time I picked up the phone I heard her boyfriend say that he had a customer, and had to get off the phone for a while. Barbara said "You go ahead and hang up, I'm just going to leave my phone off the hook. I'm really sick of people picking up the phone all the time when we're trying to talk, I'm going to teach them a lesson.

As soon as I heard one phone hang up I said "Barbara, do you want to hang that damn phone up, or do you want me to come over and have your dad hang it up for you?" Almost before I was done talking I heard the receiver slam down. I don't think that Barbara really wanted Raymond hanging that phone up for her.

* * * * *

There was another line hog who lived about a mile west of our house. She had 5 or 6 people that she called every morning, and she would talk to each one for 15 or 20 minutes. She had all the phone numbers memorized, and the moment she hung up from one call she would start dialing another number, so that no one could get on the line between her calls.

One morning a neighbor's cattle were out, and the old bucket mouth was on the line. I wasn't in any mood to play games, so I said "Mrs. Whoever, I need you to hang up the phone so I can make an emergency call, there are cattle in the road." She got really huffy and told me she had just as much right to use the phone as I did. I said "old woman, it's against the law to tie up the phone during an emergency. Get off now or I'll have the sheriff come out and arrest you."

She slammed the receiver down, I made my call and we got the cows in before a car hit any of them, but the old bucket mouth recognized my voice and she never had much use for me after that. Somehow, I didn't really give a damn what she thought about the situation.

Carol's Britches

When they were 12-14 years old, Brent Blackwell and Carol Smith used to ride around the neighborhood on a tandem bicycle that belonged to Brent's mom. If you see Carol, ask her if she remembers getting her pants leg hung up in the bicycle chain, then ask her how she got loose.

She took her britches off, at the corner of WW and Range line Road, and got caught with them off. But I don't want to embarrass her, so I won't tell anyone, unless they read this book or I talk to them in person.

Country Churches, Preachers, BAR-B-Q's and Fish Fry's

When Sis and I were little, and Grandpap and Grandma were still in good health, the family attended services at Little Bonne Femme Church every Sunday. In later years Pappy and Mom attended sporadically. One Easter Sunday the preacher surveyed the crowd, then remarked that it looked like amateur day at church. That remark made Pappy mad. He didn't get mad very often, but when he got mad he stayed mad. After that, Pappy never went back to Bonne Femme again, except to attend funerals.

*   *   *   *   *

When I was a kid we went to church at Little Bonne Femme. When Marcia and I lived in the little house at Wat and Thelma's after we got married, we attended Nashville Baptist. When we moved east of town where we live now, we went to Olivet Church, on Route WW.

We attended regularly for several years, and I did the property committee, Bar-B-Q chairman, Deacon, etc., routine. Over the years we went less and less until we finally quit completely. Someone asked me one time if we still attended Olivet. I replied "No, but I wave at the preacher when I see him, that should count for something."

I'm not anti-religion, but somehow a bunch of wild flowers or a newborn calf does more for me than an hour in church. Sorry about that, Dennis.

One Easter Sunday, John Massey, Bill Blackwell and I were sitting with our wives on the same row at church. Gene Brown came in, stopped and looked at us, then looked up at the ceiling and remarked loud enough for the entire congregation to hear, "With you three all here on the same day I can't believe the roof didn't fall in."

* * * * *

When Marcia and I moved to our farm in 1963, Burdette Wantland was the preacher at Olivet. He and his wife Shirley lived in the old parsonage, at the corner of Olivet and Turner Farm Road, and we visited back and forth fairly regularly.

One year during the church float trip J.R. Jacobs and I, along with several other people, were relaxing by the camp fire when Burdette walked up. J.R. asked "Preacher, would you drink a beer?" Burdette replied "Oh, if the supply is aplenty I would." After a while J. R. asked "Preacher, would you drink another beer?" Burdette replied "If the supply is aplenty, I suppose I would."

After supper J.R. asked Burdette "Preacher, are you ready for another beer yet?" Burdette replied "Oh, if the supply is still aplenty I believe I am." J.R. said later "Now that's my kind of preacher.

Burdette was a really nice person, and we were good friends, but he preached WAY over my head. One Sunday when he was greeting people as they left the church I told him "Burdette, some Sunday you're going to fool me, and preach a good sermon, just by accident."

I don't guess he held that remark against me, because we stayed friends.

* * * * *

After Burdette left Olivet, Larry Brown was hired as the new preacher. The first winter Larry was there, I was selling hay to Henry Forsee occasionally. One Sunday afternoon late, Greg and Jeff helped me load my old truck with hay. Monday morning I headed for Henry's dreading the thought of unloading 100 bales of hay by myself.As I came to the Parsonage, Larry was out at his mailbox. I stopped and we exchanged greetings, then I asked "What are you up too, Preacher?" When he replied not much, I said "Get in the truck." He didn't ask why, he just climbed in. As I turned south on Olivet Road I told him, "I was hoping I could find a sucker to help me unload, and it looks like you're it."

After I backed up to Henry's old shed, Larry asked what he needed to do. I told him to climb up on top and toss down the bales so I could put them in the shed. He pushed three bales off the truck one after the other, and all three landed on their corners and broke. No sooner had the last one hit than Henry came running out of his house yelling "Damn it boys, watch what the hell you're doing, I don't want all those damn busted bales laying around in the damn way." Suddenly he stopped, his face turned red and he said "Good morning, Reverend, I didn't realize that was you, how are you this morning?" Larry replied that he was just fine, and Henry turned and went back to the house.

I showed Larry how to drop the bales flat so they wouldn't break, and we finished unloading without any further problems. Henry didn't come back out, and as we were leaving I remarked, "Larry, you ought to be ashamed of yourself, it's not really nice to go around the neighborhood embarrassing people like that."

* * * * *

The first year Larry Brown was the preacher there was a cleanup day at the church on Saturday. Larry was standing at the top of the stairs to the old furnace room when Jim Moore started up the steps carrying a flat shovel with a dead skunk on it. Jim hollered "Get the hell out of my way. This is the God awfullest stinking, rotten damn mess I ever saw in my whole damn life."

Larry got out of the way, Jim went across the road and tossed the skunk, then came back and leaned the shovel against the wall. He looked at Larry, introduced himself, and said "I don't believe we've met." When Larry told Jim he was the new preacher, Jim got so flustered he just got in his truck and went home. Ever once in a while when I'm visiting with Jim, one of us will mention the dead skunk, and we still get a good laugh out of it.

* * * * *

When Dennis Swearngin was hired as preacher it didn't take him long to pretty much figure things out. One day he remarked to me "Between you, Willis Smith and J. R. Jacobs, I don't know why I even try." I replied "Hell Dennis, if it was easy anyone could be a preacher."

* * * * *

When Dennis Swearngin started preaching at Olivet, he and Sue moved into the church parsonage, west of our house. At that time Old Leon (my female coon hound) was in her prime, she rode in the truck with me everywhere I went.

One day I was headed toward town with Leon sitting next to me, with her head laid over on my shoulder. About half way to town Sue caught up with me. She said that the closer she got the harder she looked, and by the time she got right behind me she was mad. She didn't know who that girl was with her head on my shoulder, but she knew it wasn't Marcia. Sue said she thought to her self, "That's not right! Marcia deserves better than that, I'm going to talk to her!"

When I stopped at the stop sign at Broadway and Old 63, Leon decided it was time to stretch. She raised her head and shook it, and Sue told me that when those long hound dog ears started flopping all over the cab of my truck she laughed so hard that she almost peed her pants.

Sue wasn't the only one who looked twice at Old Leon over the years, before they figured out it was just an old hound dog snuggled up to me.

* * * * *

The Olivet Church Bar-B-Q is coming up the 3rd Saturday in June, as always, and I was just thinking about some of the ones past.

Cooking mutton and chicken is a hot smoky job, and it's almost impossible unless you have something to cut the smoke and grease, so we always had a couple of trucks parked close by, with enough well stocked beer coolers to complete the Bar-B-Q. Also, about the middle of the afternoon someone would always get out an old, rusty gallon bucket, and mix up a nice batch of mint juleps. The bucket would make the rounds, be refilled, and then set in the back of a truck until it was needed again.

One afternoon a couple stopped at the mutton pit on their way from the parking area, and remarked that it sure would be easier to park without all those crazy kids trying to direct traffic. They said that the kids didn't have any idea how to park cars. Someone went to straighten out the problem, and found 6 or 8 of the drunkest 12 and 13 year old boys that you'll ever see, plus 3 or 4 girls who weren't walking very good either. The kids had found the rusty bucket and the beer, and taken full advantage of both. They were shipped off to Mrs. Murphy's barn and told to stay the hell away from the Bar-B-Q until they had sobered up. By the time they got sober they didn't really feel like coming back, their day at the Bar-B-Q was pretty much finished.

Those kids have been grown for many years and several of them have raised families of their own, and I really don't want to embarrass any of them by mentioning names. Therefore, if you want to know if Mike Behymer, Greg and Jeff Easley, Randy and Brent Blackwell, Danny Andrews and Carol Showers were some of the ones involved in this little episode you'll have to ask someone else, because I'm certainly not going to tell you.

I was on the Church Board at the time, and I was pretty sure this episode would be brought up at the next board meeting, and it was. Martin Behymer was Board Chairman, and he hadn't much more than opened the meeting when one of the lady board members jumped up and said "We need to talk about this alcohol problem! It's bad enough that adults are drinking on church property, but we had a bunch of drunken children, it's a disgrace. We need to make it clear to everyone that absolutely no alcohol will be permitted at next years' Bar-B-Q." Having finished her little speech, she very self-righteously sat down.

Martin replied "I have only one thing to say on this subject. I don't necessarily approve of it anymore than you do, but before we try to ban alcohol, we need to take a real close look at who is doing the work at the cook pits. Most of the people working at the pits aren't members here; they know someone who's a member, or possibly they went to church here 40 years ago, when they were kids, or maybe they just live in the neighborhood and want to help out. It doesn't really matter why they're here, if we try to tell them they can't drink beer and they decide they'll just go home, we're going to have a real hard time getting ready for a Bar-B-Q."

Martin and I never saw eye to eye on a lot of things, and you could have knocked me over with a feather when he finished talking, because that wasn't what I had expected to hear from him. But, he made his point and I was proud of him for saying what he did, and that was the last we heard about a beer ban. However, the next year we watched the kids a whole lot closer, and made sure that they stayed out of the beer and the rusty bucket.

By the way, the contents of that rusty bucket were damn good. Just ask Jackie Glenn about the rusty bucket the next time you see her.

* * * * *

Olivet Church has been having a mutton and chicken Bar-B-Q for over 50 years now. The chairmanship is passed around, with one couple serving as co-chairs one year, and advancing to chairman the next year. Very, very few people ever want to go through that 2 year process again.

The year Marcia and I were chairman it rained all day. Of course the mutton pit was covered, so that wasn't a problem, but we had to move the chicken operation to Charlie Reid's farm. (Now Greg Michalson's.) Charlie had a pole shed which was open on one side, and the chickens were cooked in the shed, and then hauled to the church. Occasionally a puff of wind would move part of the smoke out of the shed, but most of the time everyone just stood in the smoke and worked. No one died from smoke inhalation, but there were lots of red eyes and sore throats among the chicken cookers the next day.

That was before the days of the big tent, we normally just set up tables and fed everyone out in the open. We waited until about 3 hours before serving time, and with no sign of the rain letting up, the decision was made to feed people in the sanctuary. That was long before the new pews were purchased, the ones in use were the old style, bench type wooden pews. When they were originally installed they had been toe-nailed to the church floor with 16 penny nails. We started prying them up with crowbars and claw hammers and carrying them out into the rain. A couple of older ladies waddled up as fast as they could and informed me in no uncertain terms that we couldn't take the pews outside. I replied "Oh yes we can. All we have to do is pry them loose from the floor and carry them out, it's not really that much trouble." I was not their favorite person for the rest of the day. We set up tables and chairs with aisles so narrow that the servers had to walk sideways, and hold the trays over their heads. Everyone understood our problem, and no one complained as they squeezed down the narrow aisles to find a seat. The Bar-B-Q wasn't as big then as it is now, but somehow we managed to feed over 900 people in the sanctuary that afternoon.

Early the next morning we carried the pews back in, nailed them down, dried them off and had the sanctuary ready for Sunday Morning Services. It was the best thing that could have happened to those old pews. They had been squeaking for years, but after a day in the rain they swelled up and were pretty quiet for several months.

It didn't matter that the pews didn't squeak, the two old ladies still weren't happy about what we had done. It probably didn't help when I suggested that we take them out and let them get rained on at least once a year, so that they wouldn't squeak so bad. Those two old ladies never did really like me after that, I just wasn't showing the proper respect for church property.

* * * * *

One afternoon at the church Bar-B-Q Jackie Glenn came up to me and said "Alan, we're getting behind on washing dishes, would you help us for a while?"

I replied "Sorry, Jackie, I don't wash dishes at home, I'll be damn if I'm going to wash them at the church." Jackie laughed and remarked "I always figured you were a male chauvinist." I said "Hell, Jackie, I'm not a male chauvinist, I think women are just about the best thing ever invented. Every man ought to own two or three of them." Jackie wasn't bothered by my comment, but a couple of other women who were standing close enough to hear me got a little bent out of shape.

It damn near ruined my day, knowing that I'd upset them like that.

* * * * *

Every winter for the past forty years a large group of neighbors have gotten together one evening in February and held a fish fry at Olivet Church. It's not held as a money making project, it's strictly for fun and fellowship. The fish and hush puppies are purchased and cooked outside in a large deep fryer, while the women bring salads, desserts, and other assorted goodies.

Several years ago Doc Kinkead brought a couple of pounds of Mountain Oysters to the fish fry, for the private use of the cooking crew. For the sake of the uninitiated, Mountain Oysters are plain old calf testicles, and they're the best part of the calf. However, it seems like most of the uninitiated prefer to remain that way.

When we finished cooking fish we dumped the oysters into the hot grease, then stood back to wait for dining perfection. When they floated we took them out of the fryer, dumped them on a platter and set them aside to cool a little bit before we ate them. We visited for a little while, then someone remarked that the nuts should be cool enough to eat. We looked for the platter, but it was gone. Willis Smith said "Oh hell, I took them inside with the last platter of fish, I'll go get them."

He soon returned, empty handed and laughing so hard he couldn't talk. He had gone to the table where he had left the platter, and found six older ladies gobbling oysters one after another. He heard one of them remark. "I don't know what they are, they don't taste like fish, but they sure are good." Willis just didn't have the heart to tell them they were eating calf nuts.

We all went inside a few minutes later and we had to eat fish for supper, the Oyster platter was completely empty. We never did tell the ladies what they had eaten, but when we cook something special now we make damn sure it doesn't leave the cooking area.

Damn Sewer Lines

In the early 1980s the City of Columbia ran a sewer line across the home place on Bearfield Road. I never had much use for the City of Columbia, and I didn't really want their damn sewer line running across the farm, so I drove as hard of a bargain as I possibly could before signing an easement contract.

The City Purchasing Agent was a disagreeable little asshole, and I did everything that I could think of to keep him upset. I had it written into the contract that no city employee could come onto the easement without prior permission, that gates would be installed at line fences and all cross fences for future access, and any other little nit-picky thing that I could think of to aggravate the purchasing agent.

One little item we wrote into the contract, I don't even remember what it was, the agent remarked that he had been writing easement contracts for the city for 20 years, and this was the first time he had ever written this into a contract. I replied "Hell, I'm going to tell everyone I see how easy you are, everybody will probably want it from now on." He wasn't impressed, he really didn't like me. That's all right, I didn't like him either, I thought he was an arrogant piece of crap.

Not too long after the easement was signed the contractor, who was from Oklahoma, started clearing the right-of-way. One Friday evening around 7 o'clock I was coming from T. B. Stewart's where I had been baling hay, and I decided to pull in and see what they had done so far.

Near the junction of Clear Creek and Bradford Branch was a large dozer pile full of wild cherry trees. Green wild cherry leaves are perfectly good cattle feed, but when they wilt they form Prussic Acid, and just a couple of bites will kill a cow almost immediately. It was a hot, dry summer, grass was pretty short, and I knew my cows would find that pile. I called the number of the contractor, and the number of his foreman, but it was Friday and everyone had left for Oklahoma.

I called Rodney Smith, who was on the city council at the time, but got no answer. Next I called Bob Pugh, who was Mayor of Columbia. He answered, and I explained my problem. I had a little bit of trouble making him believe the part about Prussic acid and dead cows, but he finally realized I was serious.

He asked what I needed and I told him I needed posts, wire and someone to help me build a temporary fence around the brush pile. Before to long a little short, heavy set fellow showed up and introduced himself as a job engineer for Black and Veach, who were the project engineers for the city. He took me to the contractor's storeyard where we picked up posts and wire, then we returned to the brush pile. The little guy asked what he needed to do, so I handed him the post driver. It was hot, the ground was dry and hard, and this guy definitely wasn't used to hard work, but he stayed with it until he was done, and didn't have a heart attack. I followed him with wire, and we eventually got the pile fenced.

After we finished he told me that when he got the call he thought I was just trying to cause trouble, but he said that I worked way too hard just to be doing this for fun.

The next Monday afternoon I stopped by the Contractor's mobile office and introduced myself to the job superintendent. The city had already brought him up to date on what had happened, and he wasn't really sure what to expect from me. He asked if my cows were all okay, and I assured him they were, and we visited for a few minutes, then he apologized for what had happened. He said he had never heard about wilted cherry leaves, then he said "actually, I thought you were full of crap, so I called the University of Missouri Vet School and they confirmed what you said, so I guess I need to apologize for doubting your word, too."

There were a few other incidents before the job was finished; cows getting out through temporary fences, overzealous dynamite crew, etc., but we always worked things out on friendly terms, and never really had any serious problems.

* * * * *

When the City of Columbia ran their sewer line across the farm back in the early 1980s, the Oklahoma contractor didn't originally put in much of a temporary gap at the road. They tore out 40 feet of fence, and pulled three barbed wires hand tight, with no center support. This was pretty sorry at best, but it might have worked except for the fact that Mike Martin was renting Joe Crane's old place for pasture, and they installed the same type of gap on Joe's, directly across the road from my gap. This worked for a couple of days, until the bulls discovered each other.

I got a call one afternoon that the road was full of cattle and two bulls were trying to kill each other. By the time I got there it was all over, and there were no cattle in sight on either side of the road. I patched the gaps and then went on a head count. I was short 13 cows, so I crossed the road for a look. I found my cows, but couldn't get a good count because of all the brush. I called Mike that evening, and told him that I had some cows on his side of the road. He said he was planning to move his cows in a couple of weeks, and said if I wanted to wait we would sort them out when he had them up anyway. That worked for me, so the cows stayed on Joe's place for a while.

I talked to Ed, who was superintendent for the Construction Co., and they replaced the 3 barbed wires with cattle panels and steel posts. A couple of days later the fence was down on both sides of the road, and 5 of my cows had come home. I patched the fence again and figured I'd get the rest of them when Mike got his cattle up. The problem was, when Mike got them up my 8 cows weren't there. I contacted everyone close who had cattle, and looked for tracks down at Rock Bridge Park, but I had no luck locating them.

The contractors insurance co. finally paid me for 8 cows, I purchased replacements and assumed that was the end of it. However, about 6 months later, I went to check my cows and noticed the fence was down near where the temporary gap had been located. I patched the fence, then pulled in to check the cows. Standing there with the other cows, but still staying somewhat to themselves, were the 8 cows that had been missing all summer. Their bags were strutted tight and they were bawling for their calves. They had been just ready to calve when they disappeared, and someone, somewhere, had calved out my cows and kept them all summer. Apparently when the calves were weaned the cows decided to come home.

I still don't know who had my cows "borrowed" that summer, but I hope when they decided to come home they tore down every fence the old boy had on his farm, tromped through his garden and crapped on his front porch on their way out. I don't have much use for a damn cow thief.

* * * * *

When Ed's crew ran the sewer line they had to blast rock all the way across the farm. One day I stopped to check my cows, and noticed rocks, some of them as big as a five gallon bucket, scattered all over the Northwest slope in the field where the log cabin used to be.

The next time I saw Ed I told him that there were a lot of rocks at least an eighth of a mile off the easement, that needed to be cleaned up.

He kind of grinned, and shook his head. He said he had been fussing at the blasting crew, because the grading crew had been doing a lot of jackhammer work to get the ditch deep enough. He said "I guess they decided it would be deep enough this time. I'll have a talk with them." It might have been an interesting talk to listen to, but whatever he told them worked. The rocks got picked up, and they didn't load anymore shots quite that heavy.

Ed retired after the job was finished, and stayed in the Columbia area until he passed away. Over the next 20 years we drank coffee together many mornings at Blue Acres restaurant.

He told me once that the day I pulled in at his office after the cherry tree incident he watched me get out of my truck and he thought, "Oh my God, what's going to happen now?" Ed said that apparently I had made quite an impression on the City Purchasing Agent, because he had told Ed that when he was working on Mom's place he should watch out for "that no good, hard headed son-of-a-bitch, he's nothing but a damn trouble maker." Knowing who told him that, I considered it to be a compliment.

When Ed's crew ran the first sewer line across Mom's place, back in the mid 1980s, they set the manhole tops at least 3 feet above the ground, where they could be seen, and I've never had a problem with them.

On the other hand, when Elvin Sapp ran the sewer across mom's from the Phillips Farm, he got his brother Billy's crew to run it, and that bunch of idiots set the man hole tops about 4" to 5" above the ground. That's too high to mow over with a brush-hog, and too low to see when the weeds are tall. I've mowed into a couple of them, and it sure makes a hell of a noise.

I wish Billy's idiot foreman had those man hole lids stuck up his butt, along with all the rocks they left on top of the ground. They did a really, really sloppy-assed job.

When I was a kid, anytime we sowed grass on a field Pappy always picked up rocks after it was sown, so there wouldn't be any laying around to mess up hay equipment.

When Elvin Sapp developed the Phillips property he bought a sewer easement and a water line easement across the farm. His brother Billy's crew did the work, and they left rocks from gravel size to way bigger than your head laying all over the easement when they finished. I should have taken a club and knocked Billy's whole stupid crew in the head.

Damn Trespassers

I have six signs at the entrance to the barn lot at the old "Home Place". the first one is hand painted "NO DUMPING, YOU S.O.B." Then there is a "No trespassing, hunting or fishing, under penalty of law, Alan Easley, owner", then a simple "Keep Out" sign, a "Private Property" sign, then two more on the same gate, "Keep Out" and "No Trespassing".

A while back I started to pull into the barn lot, but a car was parked in the way. They had driven past 4 of the signs and were parked in front of the gate where the other two were hung. I got out of my truck, read all six signs out loud, then asked them if there was some way I could word the signs differently, so that simple-minded people like them would understand what they meant.

They apologized and left, but there's no doubt in my mind that some other asshole is parked there right now.

The first spring after Pappy died I was patching fence at Mom's when I noticed a car parked along the road just south of the lane that leads to the barn. Shortly after I spotted the car I noticed someone walking out of the woods, heading towards the car. I reached the car just as the man was climbing the fence with his plastic bag of mushrooms.

We spoke, then I asked him if he had found quite a few mushrooms. He acknowledged that he had, and proudly opened the sack so I could take a look at what he had found. In a very polite tone of voice I asked him who I needed to ask for permission to go mushroom hunting. He replied, "Hell, you don't have to ask anyone.

The old man that owned this place died, if you want to go mushroom hunting you just climb the fence and go."

That son-of-a-bitch doesn't know how lucky he is. Mom had just lost Pappy, and I didn't think she needed to be visiting me in jail because I'd stomped someone half to death in the middle of the road, so I contented myself with giving him the worst cussing that I ever gave anyone in my whole life. When I finally got out of his face he was as white as a sheet. I've chased a lot of other trespassers off the place since then, but if that son-of-a-bitch ever came back I didn't catch him.

Years later, when Justin and Clint were 4 or 5 years old we were wandering around at Mom's one spring, when we met another mushroom hunter in almost the same place. By the time the discussion was over I had used several choice words.

After the guy left Clint said "Paw-Paw, you said some really bad words." I said "Young'un I did for a fact, but it sure seemed like the thing to do at the time."

* * * * *

If you own a farm, trespassers are always a problem. Hunter's and fisherman who ask permission don't bother me, it's the idiots who think they can go where they want, when they want and do whatever they want to do, and the hell with the person who owns the property. Those assholes I don't like!

One spring I had driven through the lots at Pappy's place and headed down the hill towards the creek, when I spotted someone walking across the field. As soon as he saw me he started running south, towards the woods. I drove as close to the brush as I could, then got out of the truck and called out for the guy to stop so I could talk to him. All I heard was brush rattling as he ran. I hollered "You son-of-a-bitch, stop so I can talk to you."

He just kept on running. I got my 38 revolver out of the truck, hollered "you better run, you no good son-of-a-bitch," and then popped off five shots into the tree tops, in the general direction that the guy was heading.

I reloaded, then went on and did whatever it was that I had come to do that day. A couple of days later I met Tom Watson in the road and we stopped to talk. He asked if I had chased a trespasser off the place a couple of days earlier. When I told him I had, Tom said he didn't know what I had told the guy, but it sure worked. Tom said he had been driving up the road when someone came over the fence from Mom's at a high rate of speed, caught his pants on the top barb-wire, fell into the road ditch, got up and jumped into his car and left in a wild spray of gravel.

When I told Tom why the guy was in such a hurry we had a good laugh about it, and decided that was one trespasser who probably wouldn't be back.

Last fall Jeff heard someone shoot from the road, just before dark. He jumped in his truck and headed down the road as quick as he could. The shooter saw him coming, and sped off. The guy slipped in the next day, found his buck, sawed the horns off and left the rest of it to rot. It's idiots like him who give deer hunters a bad name.

* * * * *

Last summer the REA line crew cut out the right-of-way on the West side of the road at the old place. There were a lot of good sized trees, and anything that was big enough to make firewood they left piled inside the fence, some of it already cut to stove lengths. That fall Jeff's girlfriend stuck her head in the house and told him that someone was stealing my firewood. He jumped in his truck and headed down the road. An SUV was leaving as he came into sight. He followed it, and when it turned east on Gans Road he pulled alongside and forced them to stop.

Jeff said, "Hey Dude, that's not a very cool move, stealing my old man's firewood." The man responded that it was public property, and anyone who wanted wood could take it. Jeff sort of came unglued, and asked the guy "between which two damn 'Private Property, No Trespassing' signs is that public property?" After a little more discussion they headed back up the road, Jeff pointed out my signs every 50 to 75 feet apart, including one directly in front of the pile they had loaded from. He watched while they unloaded the wood, and told them if he ever saw them on the farm again he would call the Sheriff.

A few days later Jeff walked into the C-store at Grindstone and Highway 63, and the guy's girlfriend was standing in line, waiting to pay. In a loud voice Jeff said, "Hi young lady, have you been stealing anymore firewood lately?" He said that was the most embarrassed girl he had ever seen, but he didn't feel the least bit bad about it.

* * * * *

After Hale Cavcey sold his cows I rented his place for pasture, until it was finally turned into a housing development. Hale's pond could be seen from Nifong Boulevard, and that caused a problem. People would park along the road, walk across the old Frank Hall Place and go fishing.

Every year before I put cows on the farm I would have to splice the barb-wires, because they would be broken from people climbing the fence. One year when I went to the pond to check the fence I just stood there and shook my head. Breaking the barb-wire and climbing over wasn't good enough for the sorry son-of-a-bitches, halfway between two posts they had cut the barb-wire and the woven wire and pulled it out of the way, so they could get in with a lawn mower and mow paths around the pond. It looked like a damn city park.

When I told Hale about the fence he said it was probably the same three guys who ran him off from his own pond. He had driven back to the pond on his tractor to go fishing, and discovered three people already there. Hale introduced himself as the landowner, then told them that he didn't allow fishing, and said that he would appreciate it if they would leave and not come back to the pond again.

Hale said one of the guys looked at him and said "old man, we fish where ever we god damn well want to fish! The best thing for you to do is get back on that tractor and go home." I asked him if he called the Sheriff, and he said he started to, then thought how easy it would be for someone to stand at the North fence and shoot 2 or 3 cows, or walk in at night and burn down his barn. Hale said he decided if they wanted to fish that bad they could just have the pond. I have my opinion of what should be done with people like that, but I'm pretty sure it's not legal.

4-H Calves 4-H Leaders

"Harg Hustlers" 4H Float, in the 1976 Boone County Fair Parade

    Some people spend a lot of money buying fancy calves for their kid's 4-H Project. Not old tight-assed me. The first year Greg joined the calf project, we walked through the lot after I weaned calves, and picked out the best Shorthorn calf and the best Cross-bred calf, which was a White faced roan.
    At the Boone County Fair that summer the Shorthorn calf was reserve champion Shorthorn, and the other calf was first in the lightweight class of crossbreds, and 3rd overall. So much for the high dollar calves.
    Greg named the crossbred calf "Chuck," after Chuck Williams. The Shorthorn steer had horns about 8" long,

which grew straight out to the side. Greg told Fred McArthur that he named the calf "Fred," because it was "dumb as hell, and horny."

Hale and Helen Fletchall were the 4-H beef project leaders that year. When Helen arrived at our place on the first inspection tour of the season she looked at Fred, then looked at me, and said "De-horn that calf!" I said "No!" She said Greg couldn't show him if he wasn't de-horned. I told her to show me the rule that said a horned breed of cattle couldn't have horns. She said the horns would come off "for safety reasons" or the calf couldn't show at the fair. I replied "Helen, the calf will be at the fair, he will still have horns, and don't you even try to puff up and pull some kind of crap to keep him from showing."

That's where two hard heads came together. I made my point, and Greg showed the calf, with horns, but Helen prevailed in the long run. The next year there was a published rule that all 4H cattle would be polled (naturally horn-less) or de-horned, or they would not be allowed to show at the fair. No doubt it was a lot safer that way, but I just didn't appreciate Helen's attitude.

The next year we sorted out a good Limosin cross steer for Greg's project. Limosin's are naturally a little quick, and they need lots of work before they learn to cooperate. However, it had been a wet spring, and Greg had spent a lot of time in the field helping me play catch-up instead of working with his calf. During the first inspection tour Greg haltered the calf, which proceeded to buck for a while, then it just locked it's knees and refused to move.

Helen snapped at Greg, "Why can't you lead that calf?" He replied that he had been working in the field a lot, and hadn't had much time to train his steer. She looked me in the eye and said "You need to decide which is more important, planting a few soybeans, or getting this boy's calf ready for the fair." I never really cared for Helen anyhow, so I looked back at her and said "Lady, I've already made that decision, that's why the damn calf won't lead."

By the time Greg got a chance to spend time with the calf it had decided it could do whatever it wanted to do. It was a hell of a good calf, and I think it would have done well, but we didn't take it to the Fair. That would have been a train wreck, just waiting to happen.

Hale and Helen raised purebred Herefords. One spring I was needing a bull to breed some heifers, so I stopped at Helen's and told her I needed a little, sort of common bull to breed heifers. She puffed up and told me she didn't have any little, common bulls. I said, "Hell, Helen, that whole pen-full would be little if you didn't have them on full feed. Those things will lose 300# in 2 weeks when you turn them out on pasture with some cows." It made her so mad she didn't even say goodbye, she just turned around and stomped back to the house, and left me standing there looking at her pen-full of fat-assed bulls. Needless to say I didn't buy one.

Leah and her reserve champion 4H ham, 2008 Boone County Fair

I've put in my time as a 4H leader, and it's really a pretty thankless job. For several years in the 1970s and

'80's, I was leader of a Machinery Maintenance and Farm Safety Project for the Harg 4-H Club. Some of the kids appreciated what I did, and a few (very few) parents actually thanked me, but mostly it was "OK, dumbass, if you want to waste your Saturday mornings that's fine, just don't bother me."

It's the same with the Ham-curing Project that I help Greg with now. Some of the kids are really into it, and they make it seem worthwhile, but a lot of the kids, and their parents, really couldn't care less.

I'm sure Hale and Helen Fletchall didn't have a very good opinion of me when Greg was in the 4-H Calf Project, so I guess it all evens out over time.

4H hams hanging in my shed. February 2009.

Grandkids

Paw-Paw and Sam, August 1999.

The grandkids were all different when they were growing up. Justin was the mellow one, whatever happened was fine with Justin. Until he was 10 or 11 years old, Clint was a disagreeable little grump. I threatened to twist his arm off and beat him with it more than once. Taylor pretty much went along with the others, unless he could think of some way to stir something up. Stephen was the most sensitive of all the boys, it was real easy to hurt his feelings. He definitely didn't like it when I called him "plumb squirrely". Sam never cared a whole lot what happened, as long as he could set and play computer games. Leah was happy as long as she had a horse. She'd just stand there and flash that big smile.

I guess if they were all alike it would be pretty boring, but at least you wouldn't have to worry about which one you were talking to, you could treat them all the same.

* * * * *

When Greg and Kadi lived in the trailer back of our house, Greg raised domestic rabbits. He had cages on the side of my machine shed, and usually had 15 or 20 rabbits.

One day I noticed that several of the young rabbits were gone. Justin was about 2 years old at the time, and one morning I asked him what happened to the rabbits. He said "Daddy bopped them on the head with a stick, ripped off their fur, pulled out their guts, and then we ate 'em." Nothing like learning the facts of life when you're young.

* * * * *

Stephen was always the most sensitive of all of our grandkids. Once when he was around 3 years old he was at our house for the weekend, and we decided to go to town for supper. When I started getting ready to go I put on a pair of jeans. Stephen looked at me and started to pucker up. I asked him what was wrong and he said he wanted me to wear overalls. I told him that Me Maw thought jeans looked better at a restaurant than overalls. He didn't really like it, but he unpuckered. I went to the closet and came out putting on a pink shirt with white stripes that I

Stephen and bottle calf "Miss Fred". November 2009.

had at the time. Stephen looked at me and started sobbing. I asked him what was wrong and he said I wasn't wearing overalls, and now I was putting on a pink "girl shirt." He didn't really get happy again until our food was served.

Stephen and Cloe, she's a good ol' pup.

Another day when Stephen was here he was doing something kind of goofy, I don't remember what, and I told him he was "plumb squirrely." He said "I am not," I said "Boy, you're plumb squirrely," he said "am not." We went back and forth a few times, with Stephen getting madder each time. Finally I said "Stephen, I'm sorry I called you plumb squirrely, you're not plumb squirrely, you're just half squirrely." That didn't suit very well either, but it's almost 20 years later and he's still talking to me, so I guess he got over it.

* * * * *

When Justin was little he went to the Bull Pen with me fairly regularly. One morning when he was about 2 years old, we stopped there for breakfast. Jackie Cockrell brought me a cup of coffee, then asked Justin what he wanted to eat. He said "Bwains and eggs." Jackie asked "You want what?" He replied "Bwains and eggs, de're good." She looked at me and asked if Justin could have brains and eggs. I told her that's what I was having, so I supposed he could have it, too.

As far as I know, the Bull Pen was the last place in Columbia that served brains and eggs. You can still find a brain sandwich somewhere occasionally, but brains and eggs are pretty much a thing of the past.

* * * * *

One afternoon I was changing the oil in my combine, and Justin was "helping" me. He was about 4 years old at the time. I was working away, and he was setting in the back of my truck, entertaining himself. After a while I walked over to check on him, and he said "Look, Paw-Paw, I greased your truck." He sure had. He had pumped a whole tube of grease into the truck bed, and then spread it around with his hands. Justin or the truck neither one rusted for a while.

Justin walked into the shed with me one day, where the combine was parked. He pointed at the sickle and said "Paw Paw, be very, very careful around that, it's really sharp, and we wouldn't want you to cut yourself." I believe that boy's Momma had been talking to him.

* * * * *

One winter when Stephen was around two years old one of my cows lost her calf. I hauled it out of the pasture and dumped it in a patch of brush.

A couple of days later Stephen was with me when I was feeding. I told him about the dead calf, and he wanted to see it. After we finished feeding I drove to the patch of brush where I had dumped it. Coyotes had been feeding on it, and there wasn't a whole lot left. Stephen looked at it for a moment with a serious expression on his face, then said "The calf's broke, Paw-Paw.

It Must Be True: Paw-Paw Said So

* * * * *

When the Grandkids were little, they always kept a pocket knife at our house. They weren't old enough to have a knife at home, but they looked plenty old enough to me.

One Sunday afternoon Justin was on the patio fooling around with his knife, and Marcia and I were in the house. Suddenly Justin came into the basement holding one of his thumbs, with blood oozing between his fingers. He wasn't crying out loud, but there were some tears showing and he was really, really close. He held his hand out and said, "Paw-Paw, I cut myself." I looked at his thumb, and it had a pretty impressive slice in it. I asked him how old he was, and when he replied 5 years old I looked at him and said "Well, I guess that's old enough to cut your thumb, if that's what you want to do."

He looked at me with an expression of total relief on his face. He wasn't all that upset about cutting himself, he'd just been afraid that I'd take his knife away because he'd done it. I patched up his thumb, and he went happily back to whittling.

That wasn't the last time one of those boys put a gash in themselves while they were supposedly under my supervision, but somehow they all lived through it.

* * * * *

When Justin first started pulling his VAC Case in antique tractor pulls he was just barely big enough to reach the pedals, but he was always wanting to go pull. He had pulled twice at Macon, on a Saturday and Sunday, and he couldn't hardly wait for another pull.

I heard about an upcoming Friday afternoon pull at Paris, so I made arrangements to take the afternoon off and go pulling with Justin and Clint. After we arrived at the Fairgrounds I discovered that their lightest class was 4000 lbs. I talked to Richard Mills of the Mexico/Paris Club and told him that Justin's tractor was way too weak to pull in the 4000 lb. class, and that we'd just watch the pull instead of entering. Richard said "Hey, that boy wants to pull, and you hauled his tractor up here so that he could pull, go ahead and unload, we'll make a class for him."

Richard said there were lots of small tractors at the show, and he asked if the Case could get down to 3000 lbs. When I told him it could he said to sign up for the 3000 lb. class, and he would talk some more people into entering. He got three other tractors to enter, and Justin beat two of them and placed second. He won $7.00, and after he picked up his prize money he asked, "Paw-Paw, we're doing alright, aren't we?"

I'd lost an afternoons work, burned a tank full of gas, drove 100 miles, paid $5.00 to get on the fairground and $10.00 to hook on the pulling sled, plus buying several hot dogs and ice cream bars for two hungry boys.

I said "Yeah, Little Buddy, we're doing alright."

Justin pulling at the Callaway County Fair, September 2000. Finished 2nd and 3rd.

Stephen and Paw-Paw, Boonville Steam Engine Show, September 2000.

* * * * *

The grandkids started going to Steam Engine Shows with me as soon as they were old enough to walk. One year when Justin, Clint and Taylor were around 10 or 11 years old they were at the Boonville show with me. They were plenty big enough to roam around on their own at a place like that, so they would tag along with me for a while until I stopped to talk to someone, then they would wander off on their own.

I had my water jug stashed under a tree about midpoint of the grounds, so we didn't have to go to the truck every time we got thirsty. Once as I headed towards the jug I saw the boys coming from another direction. We met at the jug, and after each one drank his fill I gave them a dollar apiece, for a soda or flea market junk.

After they left I noticed a little boy, probably around 5 years old, eyeing the water jug. He was wearing shorts, with no shirt or shoes, and he was covered with dust. He was sweating, and little muddy rivers were running down his cheeks and chest. When I asked him if he was thirsty he didn't say a word, just solemnly nodded his head. I said "Do you want a drink?" Still no reply, he just nodded his head again. I figured a few more slobbers wouldn't hurt anything, so I opened the spout and handed him the jug. The water came faster than he could swallow, and the excess ran down his chin and chest, making more muddy rivers. He finished drinking and handed me the jug, then just stood there as I wiped off the spout and closed it. I sat the jug down, and as I started to walk off he got a real puzzled look on his face, and asked "Don't I get a dollar?" I said "Young man you were welcome to a drink, but I just give money to my grandkids. You'll have to find your Daddy or Grandpa if you want a dollar." He didn't say a word, just gave me a dirty look and walked off. I don't know if he ever did find someone to give him a dollar.

Taylor, Justin, and Clint with Justin's VAC Case, Macon Show, 1998.

* * * * *

When Kadi and the boys lived south of Fulton, I went to pick the boys up one evening, and bring them to our house for the weekend. Justin had just gotten his beginners permit, and as we walked to the truck I asked him if he wanted to drive. He was more than willing, so we headed towards Columbia with Justin behind the wheel of my well used Dodge Dakota. It didn't handle bad, and it would stop if you had a strong leg.

Justin asked me how fast he should drive, and I told him the speed limit was 55 mph unless I was in the truck, then it dropped to 45 mph. He did fine until after we went through Millersburg, and headed toward the sharp right turn. I said "Justin, you need to slow down, there's a sharp curve up there." He said he knew, and kept driving. I repeated that he needed to slow down. He said he knew, and as the tires squealed on the pavement and Justin fought the wheel as he rounded the curve on the wrong side of the road, I said "Dammit Boy, I told you to slow down." He said, "I was trying, your brakes are a lot different than Mom's."

We made it the rest of the way home at a somewhat reduced speed, and as Justin turned in our driveway, Clint said "Paw-Paw, he did pretty good, considering that was the first time he ever drove at night." I thought to myself that if I'd known that, he still wouldn't have driven at night.

* * * * *

For 2 or 3 years before he joined the Navy, Clint helped me patch fence every spring. He got pretty good at making something out of nothing. I'd let him out of the truck with a coil of rusty barbed wire, some tie wire, pliers, hammer and pocket full of staples. When I'd pick him up at the other end, the fence was usually ready for cattle. Occasionally we'd have to go back and drive a few steel posts, but Clint could usually work around a lack of posts, unless he ran across a really bad spot.

I hope the Navy doesn't teach him that he has to do everything "just right," because I might want him to help me work on a fence again sometime, and we damn sure don't always do it "just right."

Stephen has gotten where he's almost as good as Clint at cobbling up an old junk fence. All those boys needed was a little training in how to make nearly nothing out of even less.

Once someone dumped a folding bed frame and springs out in the barn lot at Mom's. About a year later Clint saw it patching a hole in the fence. He said "The first time I saw that I knew what you were going to do with it. What took so long?"

* * * * *

When Clint and Taylor joined the Navy, Clint didn't have any transportation, and it was going to be three months before he left for basic training. I had just bought another truck to drive to work, and retired my old Dodge Dakota. I asked Clint if he wanted to use it for three months before I took it to the junkyard. It sure beat a bicycle, so he jumped at the chance. I told him the truck didn't have any rear brakes, so when it was slick he would have to slip the transmission into neutral before trying to stop. The truck had electric windows, and I told Clint "DO NOT" open the driver's side window. He forgot, started to open it, and halfway down the little electric motor finally quit completely. He drove it that way until he left for basic. When it snowed he just swept off the seat and dash before getting in.

One day he called me at work and said if anyone reported that my Dakota was stuck in a drift just off the edge of Stadium Blvd. that I should tell them that I had parked it there on purpose. A couple of people did mention that they had seen it setting there.

After Clint left for the Navy, I sold the truck to Jeff for $75.00. He traded it even up on a $300.00 repair bill he owed, then some fat gal bought it and drove it for another 6 or 8 months. I would have sworn that the truck didn't have 6 weeks left in it when I loaned it to Clint. If I had realized it had that much left in it, I would have probably kept driving it myself.

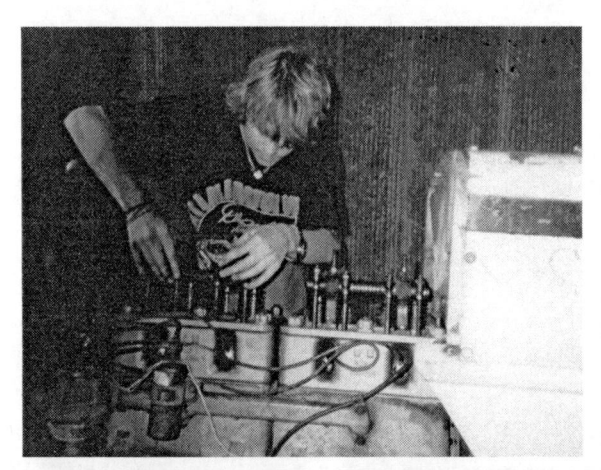

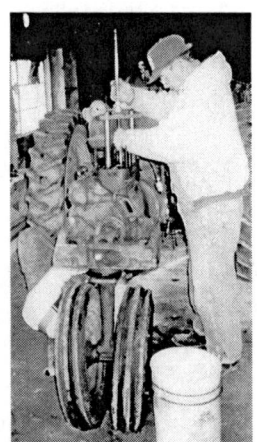

We always seem to have a project of some kind going on.

Worthless Old Horses

Charlie Hall didn't own a tractor, everything he did was with a team. Joe Crane had a Farmall "C" but he used his team as much as possible, because he said "The dad-blamed horses have to eat anyway."

When I worked for them they both tried to teach me how to harness and drive a team, but I didn't want much to do with it. If it didn't have an engine and a steering wheel I wasn't really interested.

When I was a kid Pappy was farming with a 9N Ford tractor, and was almost out of the horse business. I can just barely remember a couple of mules named Dink and John, one was white, and a couple of black horses named Buckshot and Do-Do (doe-doe). Grandpap said they had run away when they were being broken to work, and that they were always looking for a chance to run off again. The mules and the horses all died of old age on the farm.

Pappy said he had seen all the horses he ever needed to see when they used horses for farm work. He never could understand why anyone who didn't have to be around a horse would choose to do so. His theory was that when a colt was born it looked around for someone to hurt. Pappy said that the colt might die of old age without ever hurting anyone, but that it was always waiting for the right opportunity.

In the book "Swappin' cattle," by Wade Choate, there is a paragraph Pappy would have loved: "I said Don, let me hold that horse. He said "I have been roping off of Old Red for sixteen years and he's never run off." Well, sure enough, Old Red ran off and killed the calf. It just goes to show. You can't trust any horse, I don't care how gentle it is." If Pappy could have read that, when he finally quit laughing he would have agreed 100%.

*   *   *   *   *

Grandpap always worked the garden with Buckshot and Do-Do, not because they did a better job than the tractor, just because he wanted to use them.

About the only other time the old horses had to do anything was when we hauled rocks. Every field on the farm had at least one rocky spot, and some had two or three. After we plowed we always picked up rocks and piled them, and after the ground was worked we would pick up rocks again. They ranged from fist size to head size, with occasional bigger ones. After they were piled Grandpap would hitch the team to the mud-boat, which was built out of oak 2'X12's," with a 4"X4" frame around the edge, but on top of the 2"X12's" instead of under them.

Grandpap would stop the team at the piles while Pappy and I loaded the rocks, then he would drive to the nearest ditch where we disposed of them. Buckshot and Do-Do always acted like hauling rocks was really beneath them, but pulling a mud-boat load of rocks across fresh plowed ground wasn't really conducive to running off, so they pretty much behaved themselves.

*   *   *   *   *

When our Grandsons were little they would occasionally ask me about keeping a horse on the farm. I'd tell them it would have to be cut, wrapped and put in the deep freeze because Old Leon, my female coon hound, couldn't eat a whole horse before it spoiled. Then along came my only Granddaughter, Leah. "Paw-

Paw, can I keep a horse on your farm?" "Sure, Hon, will one be enough?" At one time there were 5 of them running around, the last time I looked it was down to three.

They haven't seriously injured anyone yet, but like Pappy, I figure they're just waiting for the right opportunity.

*   *   *   *   *

When Jeff first moved into the old house on Bearfield Road, his girlfriend's pit bull, Keila, spent a lot of time with him. Keila didn't have much use for strangers, but she never bothered any of the livestock.

Before Greg and Jamie built their new house on the West side of our place, Leah kept her four horses at Mom's place. Keila knew they were there, but she never paid much attention to them. One day when Greg and Leah left after feeding the horses they forgot to shut the gate. Jeff saw Greg's truck head up the road, and moments later two of the horses headed up the road behind it.

Before Jeff could get in his truck to attempt to head them off he saw Keila heading up the road behind the horses, at a dead run. Jeff said he figured with Keila chasing them this was really going to turn into a mess. As he started to pull onto the road he saw the horses coming back towards him, with Keila following.

She turned them into the lane at the barn, took them through the open gate, then stopped and sat down. Jeff shut the gate, told her "good dog," then he went back to the house. Keila had never really paid much attention to the horses, but she knew they weren't supposed to be in the road, so she got them and brought them back home.

Me, Bill, and Beer

Bill Blackwell and I drank a lot of beer together over the years. We never really set out to drink a lot of beer at any one time, it just seemed like quite often it happened that way.

Optimist Club coon suppers were always a good place to drink some beer. Tractor Pulls at the Boone County Fair, Auction sales, and road trips on Saturday or Sunday to inspect my crops all required a goodly supply of beer. Church Bar-B-Qs, late night tractor repair sessions in Bill's shop, and impromptu drive way parties also required quite a bit of beer, along with the occasional nut fry at James Earl's "Parlor."

I haven't had a beer now for nearly 20 years, and Bill doesn't drink over a couple a month, but we seem to be surviving all right without it, it's just not quite as much fun.

Bill Blackwell. Bill and I have had a lot of fun over the past 40-some years.

* * * * *

Bill Blackwell and I have been friends for over 40 years. One rainy fall Saturday back during the 1980s, Bill and I stocked up on beer and headed for a sale over towards Fulton, in my old green Ford pickup. There wasn't anything at the sale that we wanted, so after sipping a few beers we headed for home.

Just west of Millersburg we noticed an "Auction" sign pointing down a gravel road. Bandy Jacobs and Pete Kemper were calling the sale. We didn't see anything we needed, but we knew a bunch of people, so we did a lot of visiting while we sipped a few more beers. There was a pretty fair sized boat with a 50 hp Evinrude motor sitting there on a trailer, waiting to sell. It was too close to winter for most people to be interested in a boat, so Bandy started working on Bill to bid. He finally did, and wound up buying the thing for $450.00.

That was a good reason to celebrate, so we sipped a couple more beers. We finally decided to hitch up and go home, but when I backed up to the boat we realized my hitch-ball was too big. We asked everyone who came by if they had an inch and seven-eighths ball we could borrow. Finally some guy said "You boys are too damn noisy, I'll give you a ball if you'll take it and get out of here." We were too drunk to get insulted, so we took the ball, hitched up, and headed west. Two drunks really shouldn't be towing a boat down a narrow black top, but somehow we made it to Bill's, where we unhitched and called it a day.

Bill put the boat in his lake on Sunday and made sure everything worked, put an ad in the Tribune on Monday, and sold the boat for $1,000.00 before the next weekend. That's a $550.00 profit Bill wouldn't have made if we'd been sober when we went to the sale.

* * * * *

One afternoon Bill Blackwell and I were standing outside of Bill's shop planning our strategy when Raymond Smith pulled up and stopped. He was drinking a Michelob Lite and he offered us one. It was hot and we were thirsty so we accepted the offer, then opened them up and drank them down.

Raymond looked at us and said "My God, you boys drink beer, I just sip on it." Coming from a beer drinker like Raymond that was quite a compliment.

* * * * *

It seems like beer and auction sales were always getting Bill and I crossed up. One Saturday we had been driving around drinking a little beer and inspecting my crops. On our way home we noticed an auction that R. E. Voorheis was having at Harold Johnson's old place on Range Line Road. Naturally we had to stop.

It was a household auction, so there really wasn't anything that we were interested in, except that there were a lot of really pretty dishes. At least we thought so at the time. I was buying dishes for 25 cents or 50 cents a box, or stack, and what I didn't buy, Bill did. If no one bid, R. E. was knocking boxes of dishes off to Bill or I for 10 cents or 15 cents a batch. By the time the sale was over we had spent 4 or 5 dollars on half a truck load of what we thought were really nice dishes.

Doris had spent the afternoon with Marcia, so we went to the house after the sale to give our wives their pretty new dishes. They weren't really impressed with our purchases. They poked around in them with a stick, then suggested that the trash hollow south of the barn would be the best place to unload them. We would have argued about it, but they had made it plain that they didn't like the shape we were in any better than they liked the dishes, so we just shut up and unloaded our treasure into the ditch.

* * * * *

    I'd been to the beer store one afternoon, and as I passed Bill's on my way home he was inspecting his garden while drinking a beer. Naturally I stopped, and we sat down on the road bank to drink our beer. Before long James Earl Grant stopped, on his way home from the beer store. Ronnie Smith stopped next, and the four of us sat on the road bank, drinking beer and solving all the world's problems.
    James Earl had picked up some gravel and was tossing it from hand to hand while we talked. It was dry and the road was dusty, but most people slowed down when they passed so dust wasn't much of a problem, until an old van came down the road running 40 or 45 mph. As the van flew past, fogging us with dust, James Earl tossed his hand full of gravel at the van. We could hear it rattling as it hit the side. The van slid to a stop, backed up, and a couple of skinny 18 or 20 year old kids jumped out. One of them hollered "Who threw those damn rocks?" Ronnie Smith stood up and said "Nobody threw any damn rocks. You boys were going so fast your wheels threw them up and you drove into them. Now I'd suggest you get your butts back in that piece of junk and go home, and the next time you drive on this road slow down, so you don't stir up so damn much dust." They looked at each other, then got in their van and drove slowly away. Sometimes you just can't beat a good bluff.

It Must Be True: Paw-Paw Said So

* * * * *

One more party story and then I'll quit. I'd made a beer run one evening, and stopped at Bill's on my way home. He was out in the yard, so I pulled about half way up his driveway and stopped. Pretty soon the beer magnet drew another vehicle off the road, then another. About then Doris got home from work. She started up the driveway, looked at us and shook her head, then drove through the yard and went to the house. People kept stopping, and pretty soon the driveway was full and trucks were parked along the road on both sides. It seemed like everyone who stopped had just been to the beer store, so refreshments weren't a problem.

About this time Paul Wayne Garrett and Darrie Benedict came down the road with 2 tractors, a disk, and a planter, heading for the Murry Farm. They had intended to get off of Route Z before dark, but as things turned out it was after dark before they even got on Route Z. By this time the road was effectively blocked, so if someone came along who knew us they stopped and joined the party, if they didn't know us they turned around in the road and went some other way. If a bunch of drunks blocked the road today the first car that had to turn around would call the sheriff.

This thing had started around 4:00 p.m. and it was 10:30 or 11:00 before a few people finally started drifting off, trying to find their way home. As driveway parties went, this one was a huge success. I went back the next morning and helped Bill clean up the mess, it looked like two beer trucks had hit head on and exploded.

Throughout the whole evening, Doris never did leave the house and come visit us. Somehow Marcia and Doris just didn't enjoy these pop-up beer parties as much as Bill and I did.

The Fortney Cemetery

Sandy Cunningham, Carolyn Kemper and I are trustees of the Fortney Cemetery, which is located on the old Steve Sheldon farm south of Columbia. Several years ago Sandy's mom, Dell, suggested to Sandy that we needed to do a little work at the Cemetery.

One afternoon Sandy, Carolyn, Jim Cunningham and my grandson Stephen and I, under the supervision of Dell and some other ladies, met for a work day at the Cemetery. We cut brush, limbed trees, straightened the concrete posts at the entrance to the cemetery, and talked about other projects that needed to be done. We discussed a new gate at the entrance, a permanent marker of some sort, with the cemetery name and date of establishment, and fencing repairs to keep horses out of the cemetery.

Several weeks later Stephen drove 60 steel posts in the fence, and helped me fasten all the old wire to the new posts. We also spliced or replaced several barb-wires, and pretty much made the fence horse-proof again. Sandy brought a gate from his place and we wired it up 'temporarily,' until we can get a new decorative gate built. That project is still in the planning stages. (We do plan to do it eventually, if we ever get around to it.)

In May, 2010, Audsley Monument Co., from Glasgow, set a marker stone just inside the front gate of the cemetery that reads:

*Fortney Cemetery
Established 1830
Land donated by
John and Kizza Fortney*

In August, 2011, Audsley Monument Co. returned to the cemetery and reset twelve stones that had fallen over during the last 175 years, or were in danger of falling at any time.

The cemetery is far from being in perfect condition, but it's better now than it's been at any time since I was a kid. Please feel free to send money, since these projects pretty much used up all that we had on hand.

Putting Up Hay

I can barely remember when Pappy, Grandpap, Charlie Hall, Frank Hall and Doc Fortney used to stack loose hay at the home place. After that, Curt Stone baled with a mule-powered stationary baler for a couple of years. We then moved into the modern age and Raymond Myers, Melvin Thomure, and in later years Paul Riggs or David Vemer would bale with a self-tying pickup baler.

One year, for some reason, none of them could get there when the hay was ready, so Pappy got Clarence and Louise Fox to bale for him. One of the Turner boys who lived across the road from Clarence and Louise helped them.

Pappy mowed all of the hay with his 8N Ford and mounted mower, then Clarence and Louise moved in with a rake and baler to do the rest.

Everything was fine as long as Louise could keep everyone in the field, but the 2nd afternoon they were there, while Louise was baling, Clarence and the Turner boy got in the truck and headed up the road to John King's Liquor Store. They drove slow enough on the way back that they were pretty well looped by the time they arrived at the field. Clarence let the Turner boy out at the tractor and rake, then he drove on up to where Louise had been baling. Louise had been having trouble with the baler, and she had left the tractor running while she worked on it. Clarence saw the tractor and baler setting there but he didn't see Louise. In his befuddled state he decided they never would get done unless someone ran the baler, so he got on the tractor and put the P.T.O. in gear. When the baler started turning it knocked Louise to the ground and broke her leg.

Clarence knew he wasn't in any shape to drive to town, so he got Pappy to take Louise to the hospital. After her leg was in a cast and they had picked up some pain pills, Pappy started to take Louise home. She said "William, if I'm not there to watch those two your hay never will get baled, take me back to the field." Pappy took her back to the field and helped her into the back of the truck. She propped her leg up on a ball of baler twine and sat there the rest of that day and part of the next day, until the hay was all baled.

After they were finished, Pappy said "Never again." He said he would go back to stacking loose hay before he would have Clarence and Louise bale for him again. We never stacked any more loose hay, but after that if the regular baler man couldn't get there when the hay was ready Pappy just waited for him, and baled the hay when it was past its prime. He said that definitely beat the alternative.

* * * * *

When I was a kid growing up during the 1940s and 1950s, Grandpap had a good old McCormick-Deering grain binder that he always kept in the shed. Every two or three years we would get it out and cut a patch of oats. Pappy would pull it out of the shed several days ahead of time and Grandpap, who was in his late 80's, would tinker with it until time to cut. He must have known what he was doing because the old binder never missed a tie, which is more that I can say for the knotters on some of today's hay balers.

Pappy drove the 8-N Ford tractor, Grandpap rode and operated the binder, and a couple of neighbor boys and myself would shock the oats. Then two or three weeks later we would haul them to the barn for winter.

One year we cut 40 acres of oats for Joe Crane, our neighbor down the creek. My good friend Sonny Weldon and I shocked them all, because Joe wouldn't hire three friends. He claimed "one boy is a whole boy, two boys are a half a boy, and three boys ain't no boy at all."

The rest of the neighbors always paid us 75 cents per hour when we worked, but Joe only paid us 50 cents per hour. However, he was so much fun to be around that we would work for him any time we got the chance. Everyone else in the neighborhood was pretty careful what they said around "them boys," but not old Joe. He was always accusing us of slipping off and fooling around with the neighbor girls when he wasn't there. He'd say "Dad blame it boys, I know you are and I don't blame you, but I ain't going to pay you for it". He'd ask us who we were fooling around with, and when we'd tell him no one, he'd say, "Dad blame it boys, I know where there's some that look like they ought to be fooled with, if you ever get done with these oats I'll tell you where they're at." I guess we didn't get done, because he never did tell us where those girls were.

After the shocks had cured for a couple of weeks I helped Joe fill his barn with bundled oats, then we built two stacks at the edge of the field. I wasn't old enough at the time to be too concerned with how the oat crop turned out, but Joe's oats must have been pretty good that year, because he told everyone who would listen that he stacked all that he had room for outside, and had to put the rest of them in the barn.

I'd thought stacking hay was difficult, but hay couldn't hold a candle to those slick bundled oats. One stack that I built kept leaning downhill so bad that we rigged a wood frame around it and anchored it to some heavy logs with #9 wire. It stood up after a fashion until Joe finally got it fed out. I worked for old Joe quite a bit when I was growing up, but that was the only summer I ever stacked any oats. I'm glad that I had the opportunity to do it that one time, but I can't say that I'm sorry I never got to do it again.

* * * * *

When I was 11 or 12 years old, D. O. Judd got John Cavcey and me to help him haul hay for Bill Brynjulfson. We hauled from Clyde Shepard's, about where Lemone Blvd. is now, to the tile barn on the Leland Lyon's place, where Billy Sapp lives now.

Bill had a 1948 or '49 3/4 ton Ford pickup, with a 4-speed transmission. I drove in the field, and couldn't hardly reach the pedals. Those were about the heaviest bales I'd ever seen, and every 3 or 4 bales I would have to stop so D.O. could get down and load a bale, because some of them were so heavy that John couldn't lift them onto the tailgate. Usually when I would try to get moving again I would kill the engine, the truck would vapor lock, and D.O. would have to get his old truck and jump-start me.

I don't have any idea how many bales we hauled, but between a 7 or 8 mile roundtrip each load, a vapor locking truck, and 100 lb. bales, it took us three days to get finished. It wasn't any too soon, because we were all three pretty sick of that little project.

* * * * *

One year J.R. Jacobs borrowed Martin Behymer's Ford tractor and mower, so that Otis Warren could help him mow hay. They pulled in on the north end of

Russell Coats' place, that now belongs to Luke and Dee Youngman.

J.R. started around the big middle field with Otis following on Martin's Ford. J.R. was 3/4 of the way around the field before he realized that Otis wasn't behind him anymore. J.R. mowed on around the field, and when he finally caught up, Otis had his tools out and was working on the mower.

J.R. stopped and asked him if the mower had broken down already, and Otis replied "No sir, it ain't broke, but I don't know how Mr. Behymer ever got anything done, he hadn't never 'suggested' his mower."

* * * * *

In 1981 I had about 150 big round bales of Sorghum-Sudan hay that had gotten rained on 3 times between mowing and baling. It wasn't totally ditch-filler, but it sure wasn't selling quality hay.

I decided to buy around 35 head of bred cows and put them on the Murphy place to eat up my junk hay. I talked to Harold Duncan at 1st Bank of Commerce, and he said to buy all I wanted and let him know before the check got to the bank.

I went to a sale the 1st week of January, 1982, and bought 6 head. Before I made it to another sale Pappy went to the Hospital with a brain aneurism. I went to the Hospital every afternoon around 4:00, and stayed with him 'till around 9:00 the next morning. I then did my feeding and tried to get a couple of hours sleep before returning to the Hospital. Pappy passed away after 2 weeks, and it was several days after his funeral before I could make myself get interested in buying more cows.

I went to the sale barn in Columbia one Wednesday and they had a big run of bred cows. I bought 30 head, and went to see Mr. Duncan the next morning to sign a note. If anyone reading this borrowed any money in early 1982, you will remember that was when interest rates spiked. Harold wrote the note, then said "I hate to tell you what the interest rate is today, it's up to 23%." "OUCH, DAMN!!"

I kept the cows 'till nearly the middle of May before I finally sold them. I had lost one cow and her calf, and two cows hadn't calved yet, so I sold 33 cows with calves and two bred cows. The next morning I went to the bank to pay off my note, and after Harold figured the interest I gave him the check from the sale barn, and had to dig in my pocket for $40.00 to finish paying it.

I didn't bother checking all of my tickets from MFA to see how much I had spent on Range Cubes and mineral, I really didn't want to know. But by damn, I sure got rid of all my old, common rained on hay!

* * * * *

One year I was square baling hay on Sorenson's Farm at WW and Rolling Hills Road. Greg and Jeff were 7 or 8 years old at the time, and they were spending the day in the field with me. I had sold several hundred bales to Bob Klein, who had a farm south of Hallsville, and my usual crew of hippies were hauling it. After the first truck was loaded the boys asked if they could go to Hallsville with the hay crew. I checked with Dana, who owned the truck, and it was fine with him so I told them ok.

I glanced up just as the truck was leaving the field, and the boys were setting on top of the load with one of the haulers. I tried to flag down the truck, but no one was looking my way. The whole time the truck was gone I had visions of a low wire dragging them off, the truck hitting something and throwing them off, and a dozen other dreamed up catastrophes.   Actually, nothing happened, and the boys had a ball riding on top of the load, but my stomach sure was in knots while they were gone.

* * * * *

That bunch of hippies could haul a lot of hay, but it was hard to get them started in the morning. There was a dozen or more of them who rented the old Estes house on WW, just west of where the new Elks Club building is now. Some of them were a lot better hay haulers than others, but I never knew from day to day who would be on the crew. Dana was always there because he owned the truck, but other than him it was just whoever was able to get out of bed that day.

I would stop at their house around 8:00 a.m. and beat on the door until someone woke up, then I would tell them, to get their butts to the field and go to work. They would show up all red-eyed and draggy-assed , and it would take 2 or 3 hours of sweating in the sun before they got everything they had smoked or swallowed the night before worked out of their systems. Once they got straightened out they would stay and haul hay until midnight if I asked them too. Then the next morning it would be the same thing all over again. Those boys sure were gluttons for punishment.

* * * * *

One day I was baling when I noticed a dead blacksnake, at least 4 feet long, laying on the windrow. After it had gone through the baler I stopped and looked, and it had worked perfectly. The snake was almost completely outside of the bale, just held on with the twine. I adjusted it a little so that there was at least a foot of snake flopping free on each end of the bale. I rolled the bale over so that the snake was underneath, then I went back to baling.

Luckily I was looking toward the truck when that bale went on, and I got to enjoy the show. Dana was about 6 1/2 feet tall, with long blond hair. When that snake came flopping onto the truck with him he dived off the other side of the truck and landed running, with that long hair blowing in the breeze. I laughed so hard I almost fell off the tractor. I never did tell those boys what I had done. They would have killed me.

* * * * *

That bunch of hippies who lived on the Estes Place had a little bit different life style than everyone else in the neighborhood. Actually, they had a whole lot different life style.

There was a husky-built red headed gal who lived there who spent a lot of her time working in the garden. One morning J.R. Jacobs was headed to town with a truck load of wheat when he happened to glance over at the garden. Big Red was out in the garden, topless, in her panties, hoeing weeds, while a long-haired bearded boy sat in a lawn chair and picked a guitar.

J.R. came really, really close to dumping that truck load of wheat into the deep ditch on the north side of the road. He said "I bet their damn insurance wouldn't have covered it, either."

* * * * *

I was planting beans on the old Estes Place one Sunday, and Gary Chandler was disking ground ahead of me. When he finished disking he pulled the tractor up by the yard fence and parked.

No one had even dreamed of a cell phone back then, so Gary went to the house to see if he could use the phone to call Lynn for a ride home. When he knocked on the door a naked woman asked if she could help him. He told her he would like to use the phone, so she opened the door and stepped back out of the way.

Gary walked between and over sleeping hippies as he made his way across the room to the phone. The naked woman stood by the door, watching Gary watching her, as he made his phone call. When he was finished he thanked her, then went outside to wait for Lynn. He said it was kind of hard to concentrate on a phone call under those circumstances.

* * * * *

When I rented Mrs. Murphy's farm on WW, I always square baled some pretty good hay off the front fields. One year I had a lot more hay than I needed, and I was selling what was stored in Murphy's barn.

I had sold some hay to Jeff Baxter, and told him to come get it whenever it suited him. One day as I came down WW, I noticed Jeff's truck backed up to the barn. Jeff was tossing hay out of the loft, and a woman was on the truck stacking bales.

My twisted mind immediately decided this was too good of a chance to pass up, so I pulled off the road and headed towards the barn at a pretty good clip. I slid to a stop in front of Jeff's truck, as if I wanted to block it in, then jumped out of my truck, looked at Jeff's wife and said, "By God young lady, I knew someone had been stealing hay out of my barn, and now you got caught." By this time Jeff had sat down on a hay bale and was trying not to laugh out loud as he listened to what was happening below. His wife was white as a sheet, and she said in a real low vice, "we're not stealing it, my husband bought it." I replied, "Who the hell is your husband?" When she said Jeff Baxter, I replied "Jeff Baxter, I never heard of him. Where's the no good S.O.B. at ?" That was the last straw, she looked up at the loft door, and in a loud voice started calling for Jeff.

He finally appeared in the door with a big grin on his face. I said "Hey Jeff, how you doing?" He replied "Fine, we just came by to get a load of hay." I told him I had seen the truck, and just stopped to make sure he wasn't having any problems.

The look his wife gave me as I got in my truck was definitely not friendly, and the look she gave Jeff was even worse. I'm glad he had to ride home with her instead of me. Jeff told me later that it had worked perfectly, because when he pulled off the road he remarked that he hoped they were at the right barn, because he didn't want to get arrested for stealing hay.

Sometimes I won't see Jeff for two or three years, but when I do run across him I always ask if he's been stealing any hay lately.

*　*　*　*　*

One day I had just finished baling hay at Monroe Lanham's, when James Earl Grant stopped by the field. He said he had a lot of hay down, and he wanted to know if I could come over to Zane Dodge's and help him bale Zane's hay. I told him I would be there as soon as I serviced my baler. He said he was going to town, and would be back shortly.

Linda Hickam, who is now head of the State of Missouri Veterinary Department, was in high school at the time, and she was raking for James Earl. When she saw a Ford tractor and Ford baler pulling into the field she quit raking and headed over to the gate to see what was going on.

I knew who Linda was, but I don't know if she had ever even heard of me. When she got off the tractor I didn't even say "Hi", I just asked "Where is Grant?" Linda said he had gone to town for a few minutes, and would be right back. I told her that Mr. Dodge didn't think Grant ever was going to get his hay baled, and he wanted me to help. Linda's eyes flashed and she said "James wants the hay to air a little more before he bales it, he'll be here soon, and he doesn't need any help". I picked up a hand full of hay and twisted it, then said "Hell, Grant never did know much about putting up hay, that stuff's ready to bale, and I'm going to start now."

If looks could kill I'd have fallen over dead, because that girl was not happy. Linda was raking with an old 50 John Deere that James Earl had bought at Tekottee's sale. She jumped on it, shoved the throttle wide open, slammed the hand clutch forward, and popped a perfect wheelie as she headed back to the field. When James Earl got there I was baling and Linda was ramming that old 50 back and forth across the field at a high rate of speed, with hay flying. He watched her for a minute, then flagged me down and asked "What the hell is wrong with my raker?" I replied "She doesn't think I belong here, and I believe she's a little bit pissed-off about it, and she's sort of taking it out on the tractor and rake right now."

MFA
(Missouri Farmers Association)

After I decided to quit crop farming, I had an auction in April of 1994, and sold all of my big equipment. About a month later I went to work for MFA in Boonville, kind of by accident, to help them out "for a month or six weeks". It was a damn long month or six weeks.

Fourteen and one half years later after operating a spray rig, and spreading dry fertilizer on half the ground in 3 counties. I decided to retire and stay home. I'd been dragging gates open for years, but 3 months after I retired every gate on our place, and every gate on Mom's place would swing open without dragging when it was unlatched. Also, I hung gates in a lot of places where cattle panels had been wired up for years. It wasn't any to soon, things had been needing some help.

I don't know why a young man would ever choose to work for MFA as a career choice, but it gave me somewhere to spend my time, and I didn't really care about the job one way or the other, so I didn't take a whole lot of crap while I was there, but looking back I find it hard to believe that I stayed there as long as I did. Steve, you're a glutton for punishment.

* * * * *

A few years before I retired from MFA, I had a knee that had gotten so bad I could hardly function. MFA had bought a new fertilizer spreader truck, and Steve Crowley and I spent a couple of days building and installing ladders and handrails on the truck so that I could get around on it for service and adjustments.

Paw-Paw spreading fertilizer in the Hartsburg bottom. November 1999.

Someone asked Steve what we were doing and he told them we were trying to make my new truck "handicap accessible". That's when I figured it was probably time for a new knee.

* * * * *

I always thought there were some pretty good hills on the old home place, but when I went to work for MFA in Boonville I found out what real hills are like. There are hills in Howard County so steep that you could turn a team of mules over on them, and they wanted me to spread fertilizer on them.

I spread a lot of places that were way to steep to be on with a truck, and I spread two or three places that I told Mike to never ask me to spread them again, because I would have gone home before I put a truck back on those hills.

I told Joe Lee Kempf that when we took that part of the country away from the Indians I'd bet they didn't fight very hard to keep it, because it wasn't really worth fighting over.

* * * * *

I don't really think of myself as being old, but apparently some people do. A couple of years before I retired from MFA, Jamie Humphrey asked me what people used to plant corn in. I didn't understand the question, so I asked him what he meant by "What did they plant corn in?" He said "You know, back before God invented dirt."

* * * * *

When I worked for MFA, Gary Ginter liked to keep things stirred up, and I usually gave him something to stir.

I don't know who in the world told Wilmar Mfg. Co. that they know how to build a sprayer, but to me a Wilmar is the most awkward piece of crap ever put on four wheels. When I first went to work for MFA it took me a while to get used to running that floppy-gopilous excuse for a sprayer, and I didn't always do just exactly what I intended to do with it.

One of the first times I went out with the Wilmar I sprayed 40 acres of corn for Gary Ginter. No one had ever heard of GPS back then, so the sprayer was equipped with foam markers. I thought I was turning right, but apparently I was one row wide each time and Gary wound up with an 8" strip of sunflowers every 60 feet.

He spent the entire winter telling anyone who would listen about the strips of weeds that I left in his field, and how much trouble they caused him at harvest. About all I could do was listen to him gripe.

The next spring after I sprayed that 40 acres and turned in my paperwork, Mike billed Gary for 52 acres worth of chemical and application. A few days after he got his bill Gary came into the Exchange one morning. The usual morning crowd was standing around drinking coffee. Gary looked at me and asked "How in the hell did you make 52 acres out of my little 40 acre patch?" I replied "Well Gary, I listened to your bull-crap all last winter about those strips of weeds in your corn, and I didn't want to listen to it again, so every time I turned I just moved over 2 or 3 extra rows, to make sure I didn't leave any skips."

Most everyone who was standing around had heard Gary fuss about the skips and they didn't have much sympathy for him, but Gary didn't really care, he had to have something to fuss about, and the extra acres were just as good as the skips had been.

One time when I was working for MFA it had come a pretty good snow, and Jamie Humphrey was clearing the parking lot in front of the warehouse and office with a skid loader.

Gary Ginter pulled in and parked, then went inside. Gary's pickup had a bale-spike in it with the mast folded flat onto the bed floor. Jamie and I looked at each other and we both had the same thought. He said "I really ought to do it." I told him he was completely worthless if he didn't, so he eased up to the truck and dumped a full bucket of snow into the bed.

When Gary came out he didn't even glance at the bed. He had already fed that morning, so when he got home he just parked his truck and left it for the day. It warmed up pretty good that afternoon, and the snow slushed up nicely. That night it got down to 10 degrees above zero, so the next morning Gary had a solid block of ice over the mast. He had to plug in his tractor and feed with it for nearly a week, until it warmed up enough he could clean out his truck.

* * * * *

Gary was real easy to mess with and we really enjoyed doing it. He came by the Exchange one morning and picked up 50 or 60 bushels of seed wheat, then headed to his bottom farm.

He had already been by Snoddy's store and got a 12-pack of beer in case he got thirsty while he was sowing wheat. The beer was in the floor of his truck with a coat tossed over it, but the corner was showing. While we were loading the wheat we un-loaded the beer, and bunched the coat up so that it looked undisturbed.

The next time Gary came by he said "You sorry bastards, I had to drive all the way back to town to get more beer. I hope you choked on it."

* * * * *

I spread 3 acres of fertilizer for Bob Snoddy one spring, in a narrow strip between his yard and lake, and along the road. I drove a lot slower than I normally did in the field, so the foam markers were dropping plops fairly close together.

I was in the store that afternoon and Bob asked me what the gobs of pink stuff were where I had spread fertilizer. I asked "Wads of pink, foamy looking stuff, about the size of your fist?" When he told me yes, I said "Oh God, Bob, I'm sorry! I didn't know that was leaking. Go home and put your dog up and don't let him out for a week, and tell your wife to wear a mask when she goes to the mailbox." Bob was looking at me like "What the hell have you done?" when I said "Come to think about it, just take care of your dog, don't worry about your wife, let her take care of herself." Bob laughed and said "OK, Pinky, whatever you say." Bob called me "Pinky" for a long time after that.

Foam markers aren't really the best way to tell where to drive when you are spreading fertilizer or spraying, but they are always good for messing with someone.

When Chris Draffen first went to work for MFA he still lived with his parents. One afternoon I spread some fertilizer for Gerald Dick, across the road from Draffen's house. The gate to the field was right across the road from the driveway, so when I finished, instead of pulling out of the field I backed out, and backed about halfway up the drive. I switched on the foamer, and let it run while I filled out my paperwork. When I left there was a pile of pink foam about the size of a bushel basket in the driveway, with a little Dairy Queen curl on top.

The next morning Chris said his Mom wanted to know if I'd seen any pink elephants while I was spreading fertilizer in their neighborhood, because a big one had taken a crap in her driveway.

Another time, not long before dark, Jamie Humphrey led me to one of the most god-awful, desolate, remote fields in Cooper County. I would never have found it by myself, and I'd probably still be there if Jamie hadn't led me back out when we left. We finally got to the farm, I un-loaded the Wilmar and mixed up 15 acres worth of chemical, then Jamie told me to follow him and he headed across country in the old red ton truck. We drove through a patch of woods, sneaked between thorn sprouts in an abandoned pasture, jumped a few really steep old terraces, and finally wound up at a little odd shaped creek bottom.

Jamie pointed at a hole in the brush, so I eased through it, folded out the booms, and started around the field. After I got out of the way Jamie pulled about half way through the gap so that he could watch. When I got back to the gap, the front of the truck was sticking out into the beans. I didn't want to drive around it so I just raised one boom and sprayed over it.

When I backed up to turn around, I stopped with the boom over the hood of the truck and turned it on. By the time Jamie got the truck started and backed up there was a pile of pink foam on the hood, and chemical was dripping off onto the ground. We hosed the truck off when we got back to town, but apparently we should have taken it to the car wash. About a month later, no one could understand why all of the paint was suddenly peeling off of the old truck. Jamie and I had a pretty damn good idea why, but we figured it was best if we didn't enlighten anyone else.

* * * * *

When Mike Anderson worked for MFA we were always messing with each other. One day I was at New Franklin loading chemicals, and Mikey's spray truck was parked at the fuel pump. Just before I was ready to leave, Chris Draffen pulled in with his spray truck and while we were talking I casually remarked that if I had a bottle of "Bubble-Buster" I would pour some into Mikey's foam tank. Chris said there was a bottle on his truck, then he walked into the office. A quart of "Bubble-Buster" will treat a couple thousand gallons of spray solution, so I figured half a bottle in Mikey's 50 gallon foam tank should be plenty. I dumped it in, and then went back to the field.

When I got back to Boonville that evening Mikey's truck was parked in front of Gene's shop. The next morning I asked Gene what was wrong with Mikey's truck. When he told me the foamer wasn't working I said "Damn, its always something, isn't it?", then I headed to the field.

I finished all of my work sheets by the middle of the afternoon, and when I got back to Boonville Mikey's truck was still in front of Gene's shop. Gene walked across the street and said "Alan, I've changed the pressure regulator, the gauges, and the solenoid and it still won't make foam, it just pukes out liquid. Do you have any ideas what I should try next?" I told him that too much foam solution in the tank is just as bad as not enough, and I said that maybe Mikey had poured too much solution into the tank by mistake, and I suggested to Gene that he drain the tank, flush it out really good, then mix a fresh batch and see what happened. I went to the fertilizer plant for the rest of the day, and when I showed up at Boonville the next morning Mikey's truck was gone, so I guess that solved the problem.

That was way too good of a prank not to take credit for, but between a day and a half of lost spraying revenue, Gene's salary for a day and a half, plus the cost of the parts that were installed, that little caper probably cost MFA well over $1,000.00, so I figured discretion was the better part of valor and I just kept my mouth shut. Mikey always thought that I had something to do with his foamer not working, however I never admitted anything until now, but Mikey, if you read this "HELL YES, I DID IT AND IT WORKED GREAT!"

* * * * *

Spreading fertilizer is a lot like most jobs in one way. The majority of the people you deal with are pretty easy to get along with, and they treat you right. However, if you work long enough as a custom applicator, you eventually wind up spreading for a few assholes. I don't need to name any names, the ones who are assholes know that they are assholes.

* * * * *

MFA wasn't too bad a place to work until they did their big merger thing. After Boonville, Fayette, Glasgow, and a couple of other smaller locations joined together and became one big soap opera it was never the same again.

Mike Ashley left as manager, "Special Ed" became top dog, and working conditions generally went to hell. I got screwed out of a bunch of incentive pay that I'd always received, and I didn't really give a tinker's damn about MFA after that.

It's a good thing that I was almost old enough to retire when all that crap came about, because if I'd had to stay there much longer I 'spect my mouth would have gotten my ass fired, because I never was very tolerant of stupidity, and I pretty much said what I thought about some of their dumbassed decisions.

One afternoon the uniform man had left our weeks supply of clean clothes. Carroll Laurence and I had been bagging feed, but we stopped long enough to sew the legs and pockets shut on Ronnie Anderson's uniforms, that was a lot more fun than sewing feed sacks.

A local farmer walked into the mill and watched us for a moment, then asked "Alan, do you really think you should be doing that?" I replied "Hell, no more that these cheap bastards pay us we might as well have some fun. We're damn sure not making any money."

* * * * *

One spring I went to Anderson Farms at Lone Elm to spread fertilizer on corn ground. I was spreading Phosphate, Potash and a full rate of Nitrogen, so it was a pretty heavy mix.

The field joined Ronnie's yard, with just a woven wire fence between, and when I started I drove as close to the fence as possible, and threw fertilizer about 40' feet into the yard. When I finished the field I had just a little bit of fertilizer left, so I made another pass next to the yard and used it up.

Ronnie spent most of the summer mowing grass. He would mow the fertilized strip three times, and then mow it again when he mowed the rest of his yard. He didn't really see the humor in it, but I thought it was funny as hell.

* * * * *

About a year after I retired from MFA, Steve Crowley called and told me there was a truck load of junk parked near the fertilizer plant that was headed for the scrap yard. He said there were 2 David Bradley garden tractors and "Maybe some other stuff" on the truck that I might be interested in. I told him to hold the truck, that I was on my way.

When I got there Steve told me that the owner didn't want to wait, but he helped Steve unload anything they thought I might want. There were the 2 garden tractors, with a plow, cultivator, sickle mower and row marker, a pile of pretty good steel posts and a 70# IH suitcase weight. When I asked Steve how much the owner wanted for the pile he laughed and said the guy told him he wanted "more than that crap is worth, and maybe a little less than I would be willing to pay."

When the owner got back from the scrap yard we agreed on a figure that was definitely more than scrap price, but I needed the steel posts, wanted the IH weight, and could see some potential in the garden tractors, so everyone was reasonably satisfied.

I used the posts, painted the weight to use on my Grandson Stephen's pulling tractor, and pushed the garden tractors into the corner of an old shed, where they sat for over a year. I finally ran an ad in Antique Power, and sold both tractors and the implements over the phone within a week after the magazine came out, to a gentleman from Iowa who needed parts for a tractor he was re-building.

Basically, I wound up with some free fence posts and Stephen got a free IH weight, the junk hauler made some extra money and the buyer from Iowa got some parts he had been trying to find for over a year, so everyone came out of the deal pretty good except for poor old Steve, all he got out of it was a "thank you" and a chunk of deer sausage.

Random Thoughts and Other Things

The county road grader made three trips down our road yesterday, one scratching and two grading. I put the blade on my tractor this morning and pulled some gravel into the gate entrance at the barn lot and then pulled enough onto the driveway to my machine shed to fill several pot holes.

I don't know how people who live on blacktop roads keep their driveways maintained; where do they get their gravel?

* * * * *

Pappy loved pineapple malts. When I was a kid anytime we were in town Pappy always took me to the Gem Drug Store for a pineapple malt. They were the best malts that I've ever tasted.

* * * * *

When I was a kid, Grandpap always used half a corn cob for a handle on his files. It worked just as good as a bought wooden handle, and they saved a lot of injuries.

I don't recall ever seeing anyone else use cobs for handles, but I still use them when I think to save some corncobs, before they go through the combine. Corncobs are good for other things too, but I probably shouldn't go into that right now.

* * * * *

When Pappy was in his late 70's, he told me that he would never have another dog because it hurt too bad to bury them. I know how he felt.

Our little Skeeter dog died January 9, 2012, and it's a bitch, I'm sitting here crying like a baby. Skeeter was a rescue dog that animal control picked up walking the roads around Sturgeon, eating grasshoppers and anything else that he could find. We named him Skeeter because he wasn't much bigger than a 'skeeter. We had him for ten years, and he was one of the family.

Skeeter, 2008. He still has Marcia's Heart. Mine too.

He slept in bed with us, stood hopefully by my chair at every meal, waiting for a bite, and he spent his evenings laying by my chair or in Marcia's lap. When he was young he loved to chase squeaky toys, and he had a bone and a hedge-hog that he chased all over the house. He had a stroke one day that caused him to go deaf, and he never was the same afterwards. For the last two or three years he kept his toys stored side by side in the living room, next to a table leg, and he would check on them occasionally to make sure they were still there, but his chasing days were long past.

Skeeter never liked to get rained on, so I buried him in the corner of my machine shed, under the work bench, so he'll never get rained on again. We buried him with a bag of treats, so he wouldn't get hungry on his journey, his bone and hedge-hog were with him so he would have something to play with, and he took his collar along, in case he needed it. I 'spect Pappy will walk him for us until we get there.

Someone asked me if I really thought that dogs go to heaven. I replied that when I get where ever I'm going, if Skeeter, Old Leon and a few of my other dogs aren't there I'll have to assume that I screwed up somehow and didn't make it, because if there aren't any dogs there I don't know how it can be considered heaven.

I told myself I wasn't going to talk about religion or politics in this book, so I'd better shut the hell up, because I'm getting awfully damn close to talking about religion. Dennis would be proud of me.

Ol' Leon, 1989. Everyone should have one dog like Leon. We got lucky, we also had Skeeter.

* * * * *

Marcia and I started dating when I was a junior in high school and she was a sophomore. We got married the same month she graduated. We were both 18 at the time. Someone remarked that it was the youngest looking wedding they had ever attended. Joe Mahan was 20 years old, and he was the oldest person in the wedding party. On our 25th anniversary Mom said "Well Marcia, do you think maybe it's going to last?" It's been 50 years now, so it's starting to look like it might.

Young looking wedding, June 25, 1961. Virginia Easley, Martie Bishop, Beverly Arnold, Marcia and Alan, Elra Sapp, Russell Wade and Joe Mahan

* * * * *

It seems like most of the people that I'm supposed to be impressed by aren't very impressive. Is it just me, or does everyone feel that way?

* * * * *

Our daughter-in-law, Jamie, is following in the tradition of Mom and Marcia when it comes to beautiful flowers.She even has some of the original iris and daffodils from the old place.

She uses lots of rocks in her flower gardens. One December I picked up a pretty fair batch of rocks out of the creek, un-loaded them in her yard and said "Merry Christmas." It was the only present like it that she got, and she didn't have to worry about exchanging it for the proper size.

* * * * *

George Russell, owner of George Russell Farm Equipment Co. and Carver Walkup, owner of Walkup's Service Station, were two of the finest people I ever did business with. They've been pretty well covered in other chapters, so all I'll say about them here is that if there were more people like them the world would be a better place.

* * * * *

My cousin John married Charlotte when I was pretty much still a kid, so I never spent much time around John, but I remember that on the 4th of July he always brought fireworks out to the farm and shot them off. The only fireworks Sis and I ever got were a few sparklers, so that was always a big deal for us. John found Charlotte up North somewhere, where they apparently don't know very much about food. She refers to Boone County Ham as "Fried Salt," but she's a pretty good old gal, despite that. Aren't you, Charlotte?

* * * * *

Wayne Powell is Aunt Pauline's son from her 1st marriage. He and Maxine got married when I was about 12 years old.

Wayne had a bright orange Oldsmobile convertible that I thought was the most beautiful car I had ever seen. Just before their wedding he repainted the car baby blue. I thought it was ruined, Mom said Maxine probably thought an orange car was to gaudy for a married couple to own.

Sorry Maxine, but at the time I thought I'd a lot rather have an orange car than a wife. It's a good thing Wayne didn't feel that way.

* * * * *

Pappy loved to eat clabbered milk. Sometimes he would salt and pepper it, other times he would mix 2 or 3 spoons full of sugar into a bowl and eat it that way. I thought it was the nastiest looking mess I had ever seen, and I wouldn't even try it. Now Marcia buys yogurt and I eat the stuff. Figure that one out, I can't.

* * * * *

I learned a lot over the years by watching Grandpap, but I don't recall that he ever made a deliberate effort to teach me anything. On the other hand, Pappy would always explain what he was going to do, how he was going to do it, and why he thought it was best to do it that way. I hope that I have been able to pass some of that knowledge on to Greg, Jeff, and all of the grandkids.

* * * * *

Doctor's are a very necessary part of our society, but some of them take themselves a little too seriously, and it's always fun to bring them down a little bit.

Several years ago I was having a complete life insurance physical. For some reason that I don't remember it was being performed by a doctor that I had never seen before. He had done a real thorough job of poking and prodding on everything I've got that can be poked or prodded, and he was down to the question and answer session.

I was setting on his examining table in my shorts, and he was seated on a stool in front of me as he went through his list of questions. Heart attack? Stroke? Diabetes? Male pattern Baldness? Hammer toe? I answered no, no, no to his incessant questions, until he finally phrased one a little bit different and gave me a perfect opportunity. He looked at me and asked "How about sex?" I looked him right in the eye and replied "Well, I really appreciate the offer, but I don't believe I'm interested."

If I could have kept a straight face he would have left the room. He had already stood up and taken a step backwards toward the door before I started laughing. He snapped, "You know what I meant." I answered, "I know what you said, and I think I know what you meant, but these days you never can tell for sure."

He settled down and finished asking his questions, but he did move the stool back a little farther from the examining table before he sat back down.

* * * * *

February 12, 2012, I had my first spring calf of the year last night, a real pretty roan bull. It's the first calf out of my new Shorthorn bull that I bought last spring. I've been kind of anxious to see some calves from him.

It doesn't matter how many years that I've had cows, it always does something to me when I see one of those wobble-legged little rascals staggering around looking for a teat.

First calf from new bull, February 2012.

* * * * *

Occasionally having Boone County roots about 40 feet deep and being kin to almost everyone comes in pretty handy. Kevin Crane is one person that its really nice to be kin to. Thanks, Kevin!

* * * * *

Lillian Nichols died June, 2011, at the age of 95. Back in the 1980's, when both of Marcia's parents were dying from cancer at the same time, Lillian stayed with them 5 days a week for well over a year. Marcia and I stayed with them at night, her brother Bob stayed on weekends, and Lillian stayed during the week. Marcia would leave for work in the morning and I would stay until Lillian arrived. She would fix breakfast for Nanny and Paw as soon as she got there, and always fixed some extra for me.

A few weeks before she passed away she asked her son, Ernie, if he ever saw me . When he told her that he usually ran into me several times a year she said, "He sure did like my biscuits and gravy." She remembered that after nearly 30 years.

*   *   *   *   *

It seems like I just started high school a few years ago, but I guess it's been longer than that because we had our 50th re-union in 2010. Some of my class mates were looking pretty old and some of them had pretty bad eye sight, too, because I had to tell several people who I was, they couldn't see good enough to recognize me.

It's funny about re-unions. People came from California, Florida, Washington D.C., New York and everywhere in between but I counted over 15 people that live in Columbia who didn't bother to show up.

I wore my blue FFA jacket to the re-union. I wouldn't say that it fit right, but it fit good enough that I could wear it. Perk Hoecker was going to wear his to breakfast the last morning, but he was halfway to the restaurant before he remembered that it was still at home, hanging on the back of a chair.

I remarked to someone that I wondered how many of us would be around for our 80th re-union in 2040. Kathy Forbis Bryant said she'd call me, and we could meet for coffee. That could possibly be 2 more than actually make it.

*   *   *   *   *

Two of the most accommodating bankers that I ever met were Harold Duncan and Hartley Banks, Jr., at Columbia Savings Bank, which became 1st Bank of Commerce, then Centerre, Boatman's, and finally that piece of crap Bank of America. Mr. Duncan loaned me money when I was 12 years old to plant ten acres of corn. He and Hartley both told me many times "If you see something you need at an auction go ahead and get it. Just call us before the check gets to the bank. The next time you're in town you can come by and sign a note."

Now if you walked into Bank of America five days in a row, you wouldn't see the same employee twice, and if you did they wouldn't remember your name. That's just one of the reasons why I don't do business there anymore.

Years ago 1st Bank of Commerce bought the old Ward and Sublette Service Station at Broadway and Old 63 and built a branch bank.

Hartley Banks was there when the station was being demolished, and he salvaged a condom dispenser from the men's restroom. He mounted it on the wall of the guest bathroom in his "little log cabin" in Callaway County, complete with all of the comments and phone numbers that had been written or scratched on it over the years.

That's the only bathroom I ever saw in a private home that had a "rubber machine" mounted on the wall.

It Must Be True: Paw-Paw Said So

* * * * *

I'm not naming any names, and I'm not describing any certain circumstances, therefore I can't get sued for calling an asshole an asshole. However, I just had to mention the fact that there are some really low-life, slime-bag, worthless S.O.B.'s in this world. They are a total waste of hide and bone.

Don't ever try to do a favor for some rotten-toothed worthless piece of crap unless you know something about the simple minded prick.

Now that it's all over with, everyone I talk to says "Why I've known for years that worthless little bastard was crazy." I wish to hell I had, it would have saved me a lot of trouble! And $400.00 dollars.

I guess it takes all kinds of people to really make life interesting but I'll guarantee that one bottom-feeding son-of-a-bitch like him in the world is enough for everyone.

* * * * *

A few years ago one of my knees got so bad I could hardly get around on it, and I was pretty much keeping the makers of Aleve in business.

I finally talked myself into making an appointment at the Chop-Shop with an Orthopedic surgeon. After all the necessary tests and X-rays he confirmed that it was definitely time for a knee.

We scheduled the surgery, and then he explained to me what he would do, and what he expected the results to be.

By this time we had talked about cows, corn, tractors, trucks, grandkids and most everything else, and we were getting along great. He told me about several good things he hoped to achieve, and then listed a few things that could happen that wouldn't be quite so good. Finally he looked at me with just a trace of a smile on his face and said "and of course you could die, but I'd be really disappointed if that happened." I replied "I'll guaran-damn-tee that you wouldn't be as disappointed as I would."

I got my new knee installed, I didn't die, and I wish I had done it a lot sooner. I've had it for seven years now , and it doesn't hurt, and it works like a knee is supposed to work. Maybe because I had a hell of a good therapist during my rehab. Thanks, Paula.

When I was walking up and down the road every day, after my knee replacement, Jeff Bradley remarked one day that I was getting quite a ways from home. I told him I was almost to far, I needed a place to rest before I got back.

The next day there was a white plastic lawn chair out by the road, with "old man chair" written on it with red paint. Damn smart-ass! But I sure used that chair a lot over the next couple of weeks.

It Must Be True: Paw-Paw Said So

* * * * *

I'm sure there is someone, somewhere, who likes to get junk mail, but it's not me. I hate the stuff!

Depending on my mood, and how much time I have to fool with it, I'll either throw it away, return the postage paid card un-marked, or sometimes with a short "no thanks, please remove my name from your mailing list."

Occasionally, if there is a postage paid envelope, I'll stuff it as full of other junk mail as I possibly can. Anything to make it weigh more and raise the postage.

My favorite is the brick, If I'm really aggravated with some company, or if it's raining so hard I can't get out and do anything, I'll wrap a brick in heavy paper, write please remove my name from your mailing list on the postage paid card, and tape the card to the brick. By the time they pay postage on a brick they always remove my name. I'd really like to hear the comments that are made when a brick is delivered to the mail room at one of these advertising agencies. They probably call me some things that I'm really not.

* * * * *

The people who rent Cavcey's old house keep chickens. Most of the time they're in a pen, but occasionally they get out and roam around in the yard.

When Kelli's pit bull, Keila, is at Jeff's house, the chickens are safe as long as they stay in their yard, but if one flies over the fence into my pasture, Keila figures it's wild game, and it's as good as dead.

I always know when the neighbors chickens got out, because there's a circle of chicken feathers in Jeff's yard the next day.

* * * * *

One day when I was 16 years old I pulled in at Whitely Tire Co. to get a flat fixed. Bob Klein was the Manager and I'd never seen him before in my life. Shortly after they started on my tire Bob came to me and said "Son, you're going to need a new tire, that one has a bad rock cut." I told him I didn't have enough money to buy a tire, just put a boot in it. He said that the cut was too big to boot, then asked "You're going to have some money eventually, aren't you?" When I told him I was going to sell a couple of calves in about three months, he said that was good enough, just don't forget him.

He installed two new re-caps on my car, and about three months later I went in and paid for them. After that I bought all of my tires from Bob until he retired, and I sold him hay a couple of times after that.

I can't imagine a business doing that for a 16 year old kid today and I suppose there are a lot of reasons why they shouldn't, but it sure made for a good long-term relationship.

* * * * *

After Bill Blackwell retired from the University, he and Bev moved back to his old hometown of Doniphan, so they could be closer to Bill's mother.

I'm not really much of a traveler, but Marcia and I went to visit them a couple of times over the years. The last time we were there we took a pretty round-a-bout route coming back, and stopped at Museums, Old Mills, etc., as we made our way home.

The last day we were a few miles north of Rolla, on the crooked, hilly, two lane section of Highway 63 that still hasn't been re-placed. Suddenly, on a curve at the top of a hill, two cars appeared side by side, as some idiot attempted to pass. There aren't any shoulders on that road, but I squeezed one way as far as I could, the car being passed squeezed the other way, and the dumbass that caused it went down the middle. It was probably as close as I've ever come to being in a wreck without it actually happening.

About an hour later we were headed north from Jefferson City, on a flat, straight section of four lane road, when I pulled out to pass a tractor-trailer. As I got even with the trailer axles a tire blew out on an outside dual, splattering the side of our car with dust, dirt and chunks of rubber. I told Marcia "to hell with this, someone is trying to tell us something, when we get to the Airport road I'm getting off, I've had all of Highway 63 I want for one day."

We took the back roads for the last ten miles or so, and made it home without any further incident, and when I checked the side of the car it had some black marks on it from the rubber, but there weren't any dents. However, two scares like that, within an hour of each other was almost enough to get me back to church. Almost, but not quite.

The first time we went to Doniphan to visit Bill and Bev, Bev had some really pretty flowers, but she said it was kind of discouraging trying to grow flowers in flint rocks and red clay.

When we got home I called Bill's oldest son, Randy, and told him I had something for him to take to Bev the next time he went to see them. He came by a couple of weeks later, and I sent him on his way with two feed sacks full of dirt.

I feed big round bales in a different location each year, and by the second year the cow poop and left-over hay is rotted down into the richest, blackest, most weed-infested dirt you'll ever run across. Bev was tickled to death with the dirt, even if she did have to pull a lot of weeds for a while.

* * * * *

Apparently the latest thing everyone is supposed to be worried about is getting sick from E coli. Hell, when I was a kid, if a fly fell into the milk bucket while I was milking I'd try to hit it with the next stream and sink it. Mom or Grandma always strained the milk anyhow, and the strainer took out all of the dead flies, tail hairs and little chunks of anything else that had gotten into the bucket while we were milking, and I don't remember anyone ever getting sick from drinking contaminated milk.

In later years when Doc Kinkead would work cattle for me, he would castrate, vaccinate, maybe de-horn a few calves, and sometimes pregnancy check my cows. If he wanted a fresh chew of Skoal while he was working and there wasn't any water handy to wash up with, I've seen him more than once sniff his fingers and then get a chew with the two fingers that smelled the best. I can't tell that it hurt him much, he's still going strong, so I don't think that I'm going to lose a whole lot of sleep worrying about E Coli.

* * * * *

I rented the Murphy farm at WW and Olivet Road for 25 years. The whole time I rented Murphy's I always thought that It would be nice to rent Brown's, put a gate in the fence and run cattle on both places. Of course when I was renting Murphy's Gene Brown had his own cattle and the place wasn't available.

After I went to work for MFA in Boonville the farm became available for rent, but I had gotten rid of 40 head of cows. and dropped all of my rented ground except Mom's Place, and I wasn't interested in more pasture at that time.

In November, 2011, the man who was renting Brown's told me that he had bought a farm and would be moving his cattle at the end of the year. So what did I do? I called Marilyn and rented the farm. By the time I get cattle moved onto the place I'll be 70 years old, and I don't know why in the hell I wanted another 60 acres of pasture with old fence, but I've got it and we'll see what happens. No one ever accused me of having good sense.

* * * * *

It didn't matter what you had, Raymond Myers always had one that was a little bit better. If you had been standing in your front yard with Raymond, looking at a stump, he would have said "By God, that's a pretty good stump, but I've got one in my yard that's better".

I always liked to go to the Bull Pen when Raymond was there, because it was so easy to bait him a little bit and get him stirred up. I'd listen for a while, and whatever he was talking about I'd take a completely opposite viewpoint, and start arguing with him. One day he was wound up about school taxes. He thought people without kids shouldn't have to pay school tax. I said, " Hell Raymond, people like me, with kids, have plenty to spend our money on. We have to buy them food, clothes, pay their doctor bills, and lots of other stuff. We have enough to spend our money on without paying taxes. People without kids don't have anything to spend money on if you don't use it to pay taxes you're just going to waste it. I think people without kids should have their school tax doubled."

The longer I'd talked to madder Raymond had gotten, and when I finished that last sentence he said "Well, By God!" He slammed his coffee cup down on the table, then got up and went to the far end of the restaurant, sat down at another table, and ordered more coffee. I almost overdid it that time, it was 2 or 3 weeks before Raymond would set at the same table with me again.

* * * * *

The idiots that run the Boone County government act like we're in the middle of New York City, instead of a semi-rural county. The only governing body I know of that is more screwed up than Boone County is the City of Columbia.

There are so damn many dumbassed rules and regulations that it's almost impossible to do anything. They make it so hard to sell a piece of property that it's not hardly worth the trouble. The next thing you know the butt heads will try to make it illegal to stand in your own back yard and take a leak.

Marcia says I'm just getting grumpy in my old age. I told her I don't see much chance of that getting any better in the for-seeable future.

* * * * *

Marcia's dad worked as plumbing foreman for J. Louis Crum Corp. for many years. I joined Plumbers and Pipefitters Local 317, and worked construction for 10-15 years after Marcia and I got married. An old welder that I worked with had a saying: "If it smells like bullshit and tastes like bullshit, it's probably bullshit." You can look at some people and pretty much tell what it's going to smell like, before they ever start talking.

* * * * *

July 4, 2012, the driest summer we've had since 1980. I'm setting out by the barn at Marilyn Brown's, filling water tanks for my cows, because the ponds went dry.

West of Marilyn's, northwest, and to the south between Marilyn's and the church fire crackers are going off. The idiots won't be happy until they burn up the whole country.

I know God made lots of stupid people, but I don't know why they all want to live in Boone County.

* * * * *

Late July, 2012, right in the middle of one of the hottest, driest summers on record, I ordered a couple of loads of gravel for the barn lot. I put the blade on the tractor and pushed it around the best that I could. When I went to the house Marcia asked me if I was finished. I told her I had a little hand work to do, but I thought I'd wait and do it some other time.

A couple of hours later she saw me walking across the yard with a rake on my shoulder. When she asked me what I was doing. I replied that I was going to finish smoothing out the gravel. She said, "Mister, it's 105 degrees, and you're 70 years old!" I said "That's why I'm going to do it now, before it gets too hot, or I get too old."

I ordered 1" gravel for the barn lot. I guess as dry as it's been I should have ordered 2" instead. I lost half a load down the cracks in the ground before it ever piled up enough I could blade it around.

* * * * *

August 12, 2012, I just read in the Sunday paper that Larry Winfrey passed away. Damn! The Good Old Boys are getting fewer every day. Larry was raised just west of Wat Cheavens' place, and I've known him all of my life.

After Larry retired he started sharpening saw chains, sort of as a hobby, and he sure 'nuff could sharpen them better than anyone else around. I was always glad when I had a couple of dull chains, it gave me a good excuse to go visit Larry for a while.

* * * * *

My cousin Burdette Cheavens passed away on November 11, 2012. I was visiting with his son, Steve, a couple of days before the funeral, when we realized that I'm now the oldest surviving male member of the Easley, Cheavens and Hall Families. I've got a bunch of sweet little girl cousins, who judging by their looks are all much, much, much younger than me, but I'm the oldest male left. That is scary! It doesn't seem like its been that many years since I was one of the youngest. I've got a whole bunch of stuff left that I still want to do, but it looks like I'm going to be old as hell before I manage to get it all done.

* * * * *

Years ago an old fella down near McBaine married a much younger woman. Several of his friends were riding him pretty hard about "taking care of business." He finally told them "By God boys, I's jist a doin' all I kin do!"

That's kind of how I am with this book. If you don't like what I've written I'm sorry, but "I's jist a doin' all I kin do!" I never said I was good.

*   *   *   *   *

Everything that I've written about in this book actually happened. If anyone reads something about themselves that offends them, too bad. They should have thought about what they were doing before they did it.

Well that's all there is. This mixture of stuff just popped into my head from time to time, and I jotted it down before I forgot it again. I hope you enjoyed it. There is some other stuff that I'm sure you would enjoy, but I can't tell it, too many people are still alive. Maybe someday.